Why We Love Sociopaths

A Guide to Late Capitalist Television

Why We Love Sociopaths

A Guide to Late Capitalist Television

Adam Kotsko

Winchester, UK
Washington, USA

First published by Zero Books, 2012
Zero Books is an imprint of John Hunt Publishing Ltd., Laurel House, Station Approach,
Alresford, Hants, SO24 9JH, UK
office1@o-books.net
www.o-books.com

For distributor details and how to order please visit the 'Ordering' section on our website.

ISBN: 978 1 78099 091 0

A CIP catalogue record for this book is available from the British Library.

Design: Lee Nash

Printed in the UK by CPI Antony Rowe
Printed in the USA by Offset Paperback Mfrs, Inc

We operate a distinctive and ethical publishing philosophy in all
areas of our business, from our global network of authors to
production and worldwide distribution.

CONTENTS

Acknowledgments

I'd like to thank the following people who have helped me with this project, either through talking through the ideas with me or reading drafts: Natalie Scoles, Brad Johnson, Erika Bolden, Ted Jennings, and Tariq Goddard. I'd also like to thank everyone involved at Zer0 Books for publishing a second book of mine in their excellent series.

Portions of chapter 3 first appeared in a slightly different form in "The Ethics of Dr. Gregory House," *PopMatters*, April 23, 2009 <http://www.popmatters.com/pm/feature/the-ethics-of-dr.-gregory-house/>.

Introduction

On the desire to be a sociopath

My greatest regret is that I'm not a sociopath. I suspect I'm not alone. I have written before that we live in the age of awkwardness, but a strong case could be made that we live in the age of the sociopath. They are dominant figures on television, for example, and within essentially every television genre. Cartoon shows have been fascinated by sociopathic fathers (with varying degrees of sanity) ever since the writers of *The Simpsons* realized that Homer was a better central character than Bart. Showing that cartoon children are capable of radical evil as well, Eric Cartman of *South Park* has been spouting racial invective and hatching evil plots for well over a decade at this point. On the other end of the spectrum, the flagships of high-brow cable drama have almost all been sociopaths of varying stripes: the mafioso Tony Soprano of *The Sopranos*, the gangsters Stringer Bell and Marlo of *The Wire*, the seductive imposter Don Draper of *Mad Men*, and even the serial-killer title character of *Dexter*. In between, one might name the various reality show contestants betraying each other in their attempt to avoid being "voted off the island"; Dr. House, who seeks a diagnosis with complete indifference and even hostility toward his patients' feelings; the womanizing character played by Charlie Sheen on the sitcom *Two and a Half Men*; Glenn Close's evil, plotting lawyer in *Damages*; the invincible badass Jack Bauer who will stop at nothing in his sociopathic devotion to stopping terrorism in *24* — and of course the various sociopathic pursuers of profit, whether in business or in politics, who populate the evening news.

On a certain level, this trend may not seem like anything new. It seems as though most cultures have lionized ruthless individuals who make their own rules, even if they ultimately feel constrained to punish them for their self-assertion as well. Yet there is something new going on in this entertainment trend that goes beyond the understandable desire to fantasize about living without the restrictions of society. The fantasy sociopath is somehow outside social norms—largely bereft of human sympathy, for instance, and generally amoral—and yet is simultaneously a master manipulator, who can instrumentalize social norms to get what he or she wants.

It is this social mastery that sets the contemporary fantasy sociopath apart from both the psychopath and the real-life sociopath. While many of the characters named above are ruthless killers, they are generally not psychopathic or "crazy" in the sense of seeking destruction for its own sake, nor do they generally have some kind of uncontrollable compulsion to struggle with. Indeed, they are usually much more in control of their actions than the normal "sane" person and much more capable of creating long-term plans with clear and achievable goals.

This level of control also sets them apart from a more clinical definition of sociopathy. I do not wish to delve into the *DSM* or any other authority in the field of psychology, where the usefulness of sociopathy as a diagnostic category is in any case disputed. Yet as I understand it, real-life sociopaths are pitiable creatures indeed. Often victims of severe abuse, they are bereft of all human connection, unable to tell truth from lies, charming and manipulative for a few minutes at most but with no real ability to formulate meaningful goals. The contemporary fantasy of sociopathy picks and chooses from those characteristics, emphasizing the lack of moral intuition, human empathy, and emotional connection. Far from being the obstacles they would be in real life, these characteristics are what enable the fantasy sociopath to be so amazingly successful.

It is curious to think that power would stem so directly from a lack of social connection. After all, we live in a world where we are constantly exhorted to "network," to live by the maxim that "it's all about who you know." Yet the link between power and disconnection is a persistent pattern in recent entertainment, sometimes displayed in the most cartoonish possible way. Take, for instance, Matt Damon's character in the various Bourne movies (*The Bourne Identity*, *The Bourne Supremacy*, and *The Bourne Ultimatum*— soon to be followed, as Damon has joked, by *The Bourne Redundancy*). In the first film, Jason Bourne is fished out of the ocean with no idea of who he is. As the story unfolds, he finds that he is unexpectedly the master of everything he tries to do: from hand-to-hand combat, to stunt driving, to speaking apparently every language on earth. His skills apply interpersonally as well, as the very first woman he meets (Franka Potente) becomes his partner in crime and then lover.

The narrative explanation for Bourne's near superhero status is an elite CIA training program. Yet that training is directly tied to Bourne's amnesia, as the program's goal is to create the ultimate "sleeper" agents. The program culminates with a thorough brainwashing, after which the agents don't remember they're agents until their programming is triggered by some signal. The life the CIA sets up for the agent is, in true sociopathic style, only an act that can be left behind at any time. What's more, a later film reveals that Bourne's trainers only regarded him as truly ready to work once they had induced him to kill in cold blood someone he believed to be an innocent man. Lack of social ties and ruthless amorality thus fit together seamlessly with virtual superpowers in this movie.

The pattern isn't limited to superheroes. For instance, Don Draper of *Mad Men*, arguably the most iconic and exemplary contemporary TV sociopath, becomes a powerful ad executive who appears to do little but drink all day and wait for random flashes of inspiration. And as if securing a wife who looks like Grace Kelly isn't enough, he repeatedly seduces interesting, substantial women, because for most of the series' run, the standard route of seducing naïve young secretaries is simply beneath him. What enabled this miraculous rise? Stealing the identity of a man who has literally just died in front of him and then abandoning his family!

Many of these sociopathic characters are, of course, "psychologically complex," particularly in shows with high-brow ambitions. Don Draper is never sure what he wants, though he nearly always gets it, and Tony Soprano famously seeks out therapy to help him deal with the stress of being a mob boss. Dexter gets a voiceover where he muses about what it must be like to feel sympathy or happiness or sadness, while House is subjected to endless amateur psychoanalysis by his friends and co-workers, distraught about how he can be so rude and cynical.

It is hard to believe, however, that the exploration of the dark side of the human psyche for its own sake is behind the appeal of these sociopathic characters. What, then, is going on in this trend? My hypothesis is that the sociopaths we watch on TV allow us to indulge in a kind of thought experiment, based on the question: "What if I really and truly did not give a fuck about anyone?" And the answer they provide? "Then I would be powerful and free."

In order to get at why this thought experiment would be appealing, and even more why this somewhat counter-intuitive answer would be compelling, I believe it will be helpful to take a detour through awkwardness.

Sociopathy as reverse awkwardness

At first glance, the TV sociopath appears to be nearly the opposite of the awkward character. I've previously defined awkwardness as the feeling of anxiety that accompanies the violation or absence of a clear social norm. It could happen when someone commits a social *faux pas*, such as telling a racist joke (what I've called "everyday awkwardness"), or it could occur in situations where there are no real social expectations to speak of—for instance, in cross-cultural encounters where one cannot appeal to a third "meta-culture" to mediate the interaction (what I've called "radical awkwardness"). In both cases, we are thrown into a situation in which we don't know what to do. At the same time, however, this violation or lack of social norms doesn't simply dissolve the social bond. Instead, awkwardness is a particularly powerful social experience, in which we feel the presence of others much more acutely—and more than that, awkwardness *spreads*, making even innocent bystanders feel somehow caught up in the awkward feeling. This "raw" feeling of social connection can be so anxiety-producing, in fact, that I have even hypothesized that awkwardness comes first and social norms are an attempt to cope with it.

In contrast to the sociopath, then, whose lack of social connection makes him or her a master manipulator of social norms, people caught up in awkwardness are rendered powerless by the intensity of their social connection. Thus we might say that at second glance, the TV sociopath is the *exact* opposite of the awkward character—the correspondence is too perfect to ignore.

To understand why this connection might exist, I'd like to look more closely at my distinction between the violation and the lack of a social norm. The distinction between these two situations is not hard and fast, because in many cases, it's not clear how to react to the violation of a social norm. Many social norms function as straightforward commandments—for example, "thou shalt not take cuts in line"—but fail to prescribe a punishment or designate an agent who is qualified to administer it. As a result, when someone does take cuts, there seems to be nothing anyone can do.

In fact, the person who does decide to confront the offender may well come out looking like the asshole in the situation, because in many cultural settings there is a strong bias against

5

unnecessary confrontation. The awkward person sits and fumes, or else confronts the cutter and quickly retreats. If we could define something like the everyday sociopath, it would be the person who is not only callous enough to take cuts in the first place, but is able to manipulate social expectations to shame the person who calls out the violation.

The transition to the fantasy of TV sociopathy comes when the awkward person shifts from "I hate that guy" to "I wish I were that guy." In everyday settings, this shift is unlikely. Even if the line is unbearably long, most well-adjusted people would prefer not to disobey their ingrained social instincts and, if confronted with a queue-jumper, would console themselves with the thought that at least *they* are not such inconsiderate people, etc. Similar patterns repeat themselves in other areas of life—a man may wish, for instance, that he were a suave seducer, but at bottom he feels that the seducer is really a douche bag. Even though envy is probably inevitable, a feeling of moral superiority is normally enough to stave off outright *admiration* of the everyday sociopath.

In order to get from the everyday sociopath to the fantasy sociopath, we need to think in terms of my third class of awkwardness, which I've called cultural awkwardness, but perhaps should have called *culture-wide* awkwardness. Falling in between the types of awkwardness stemming from a violation and a lack of a social norm, cultural awkwardness arises in a situation where social norms are in the process of breaking down. Just as it's easier to criticize than to create, a social order in a state of cultural awkwardness is perfectly capable of telling us what we're doing wrong—but it has no convincing account of what it would look like to do things right. My favorite encapsulation of this Kafkaesque logic remains a quote from Gene Hackman's character in *Royal Tenenbaums*: "It's certainly frowned upon, but then what isn't these days?"

In *Awkwardness*, I argued that the proper response to our culture-wide awkwardness is simply to embrace rather than try to avoid awkwardness. After all, if the social bond of awkwardness is more intense than our norm-governed social interactions, it also has the potential to be more meaningful and enjoyable. Such a strategy sacrifices comfort and predictability, but it's not clear that comfort and predictability in our interactions are always desirable anyway.

What our cultural fascination with the fantasy sociopath points toward, however, is the fact that the social order doesn't exist simply to provide comfort and predictability in interpersonal interactions. One would hope that it might also deliver some form of justice or fairness. The failure to deliver on that front is much more serious and consequential than the failure to allay our social anxieties, though the pattern is similar in both cases. In a society that is breaking down, the no-win situation of someone flagrantly cutting in line repeats itself over and over, on an ever grander scale, until the people who destroyed the world economy walk away with hundreds of millions of dollars in "bonuses" and we're all reduced to the pathetic stance of fuming about how much we hate that asshole—and the asshole also has the help of a worldwide media empire (not to mention an increasingly militarized police force) to shout us down if we gather up the courage to complain.

At that point, the compensation of moral superiority no longer suffices. We recognize our weakness and patheticness and project its opposite onto our conquerors. If we feel very acutely the force of social pressure, they feel nothing. If we are bound by guilt and obligation, they are completely amoral. And if we don't have any idea what to do about the situation, they always know *exactly* what to do. If only I didn't give a fuck about anyone or anything, we think—then I would be powerful and free. Then I would be the one with millions of dollars, with the powerful and prestigious job, with more sexual opportunities than I know what to do with. In short order, it even comes to seem that *only* such people can get ahead.

This interpretation has much to recommend it. The people who run our world do a lot of terrible things, and the highest level of contrition they display is seldom more than a token gesture—in fact, officials regularly "take full responsibility" for things without suffering any apparent consequences at all. It takes a special kind of person to order the invasion of a country with no provocation, to cut social programs that millions rely on in order to meet the demands of bondholders, or to deprive people of their livelihood because a set of numbers isn't adding up in the right way. One can easily argue that the various managers and administrators who control our lives are overpaid, but the callousness they routinely display really does represent a rare skill set. I know that I couldn't cope with the guilt if I behaved like them—right?

Yet perhaps I could. Perhaps the problem isn't that we're being ruled by sociopathic monsters, but rather by people who are just as susceptible to social forces as the rest of us. One might think here of the frequently observed phenomenon of people being perfectly nice one-on-one, but obnoxious and unbearable when part of a group—something often associated with gender-segregated adolescent groups.

Individual members of a fraternity or sports team, for example, might be uncomfortable with the way they are expected to behave toward women—they might have a less constrained view of who counts as "attractive" or be uncomfortable with hook-up culture—but they conform in order to avoid getting made fun of by the other guys. And why will those other guys make fun of them? Because *they* will be made fun of if they take the non-conformist's side. The dynamic whereby these young men have to continually prove that they're "real men" or else face ostracization doesn't require any individual young man to be a bad person going in. And though the addition of a genuinely malicious person might exacerbate the problem, the dynamic is basically self-sustaining without the need for any external "evil" inputs.

Similar dynamics obviously happen in the corporate and political worlds as well, particularly in light of how insular those social circles can be. A politician must be willing to make "tough choices"—and somehow that tough choice is always somehow related to piling further burdens on the already disadvantaged. Of course no one wants to be a bleeding heart, or an idealist, or a wimp, and so no one seriously pushes back. Yet all these spineless conformists style themselves, à la John McCain, as straight-shooting mavericks who aren't afraid to tell it like it is.

For every average Joe saying to himself, "I wish I was like Tony Soprano," then, there's a member of the ruling class saying to himself, "You know, *I am* kind of like Tony Soprano—it's not always pretty, but I do what needs to be done." What both fail to recognize is that Tony Soprano's actions are no more admirable or necessary than the decision to exclude some poor schlub from the in-group on the playground. More fundamentally, both fail to recognize that what is going on is a *social* phenomenon, a dynamic that exceeds and largely determines the actions of the individuals involved—not a matter of some people simply being more callous or amoral (though some people certainly are) *or* being more clear-eyed and realistic (as few of us really are in any serious way).

Love and other market forces

The fantasy of the sociopath, then, represents an attempt to escape from the inescapably *social* nature of human experience. The sociopath is an individual who transcends the social, who is not bound by it in any gut-level way and *who can therefore use it* purely as a tool. The two elements of the fantasy sociopath may not make for a psychologically plausible human being, but they are related in a rigorously consistent way.

Indulging in the fantasy of the sociopath is thus the precise opposite of the strategy of indulging in the primordial social experience of awkwardness. Both approaches, however, respond to the same underlying reality, which is a social order that is breaking down, making impossible demands while failing to deliver on its promises. As such, both testify to the value of the social insofar as they mourn its collapse.

This mourning is evident in the various morality plays that often surround the fantasy of the sociopath. These morality plays acknowledge that the sociopath's greatest strength is his social disconnection, but they then make it into his greatest weakness. (It normally is "his," as women's still-subordinate place in the social hierarchy gives them the unavoidable knowledge of social forces that comes from being on their receiving end.) The goal becomes making a meaningful social connection, in the recognition that the sociopath is not really a full human being. Once this quest is undertaken, the two options seem to be that the sociopath either does succeed in making a connection and thus redeems himself by mitigating his sociopathy, or else he fails to make that connection and experiences this failure as a kind of punishment, so that his sociopathy feels like a trap.

The first option is a long-standing tradition, going back to Charles Dickens' *Christmas Carol* and beyond. The second option, though, seems to me to be more interesting and more characteristic of the current fascination with sociopaths. A good example of this "punishment" model is the film *Up in the Air*. In it, George Clooney plays a totally disconnected man with the ghastly job of flying around the country and firing people on behalf of managers who can't bear the emotional burden. He loves the lifestyle of constant travel, the perks that come with having millions of frequent-flyer miles, the casual hook-ups with fellow-travelers—and above all the ability to carry around his entire life with him in a single suitcase. He is also amazingly skilled at emotional manipulation, convincing worker after worker that the loss of this job is actually the greatest opportunity they've ever received, as now they can begin following their dreams.

Demonstrating that he is a true believer in what he does, he even has a successful career as a motivational speaker, encouraging others to adopt his philosophy of "travelling light."

The main conflict in the story comes from a young woman (Anna Kendrick) who comes up with a way to eliminate the need for constant travel, instead administering the firings via video-conference. Obviously this method is even more inhuman than what it's replacing, so she at first seems to be even more socio-pathic than George Clooney himself. The twist, however, comes when she convinces him that a woman with whom he has a regular hook-up arrangement (Vera Farmiga) must—as stereotype would dictate—be merely tolerating their set-up and really want "more." Clooney follows up on this by inviting Farmiga to his sister's wedding, where he is paradoxically called upon to convince a groom with cold feet of the value of marriage. Apparently buying his own pitch, he decides to pursue a more serious relationship with his hook-up partner, only to learn that she's already married with a family.

After that disappointment, his achievement of reaching ten million frequent-flyer miles—up until then apparently his only major life goal—feels hollow. His only consolation is to make some attempt to reach out to people sincerely (by giving Anna Kendrick a glowing letter of recommendation, for instance, or transferring some of his miles to his sister and her new husband, who can't afford to travel).

To me, this ending feels artificial and unsatisfying—it would've been more interesting had George Clooney stuck to his principles. At the same time, however, the ending was *culturally* necessary, as it seems nearly impossible for mainstream enter-tainment (and even much "high-brow" material) to present a sociopathic character without staging some kind of confrontation with the "true humanity" of deep human connection. And with very few exceptions, this deep human connection is represented by marriage and family, rather than by close friendship, for example.

This contrast between family values and sociopathy at first seems relatively intuitive, but I think something more subtle is going on. The reference to family does not undermine the fantasy of the sociopath, but instead maintains it while providing the "plausible deniability" of a moral lesson. This is clearest in the punishment model, where the sociopath remains irreducibly sociopathic despite the supposedly obvious appeal of family life. Yet I would contend that it's still at work in the redemption model, and this is because family connections are completely compatible with sociopathy. Indeed, as later chapters will show, family dynamics provide remarkably productive ways for describing how the fantasy of the sociopath operates.

Bryan Cranston's character in *Breaking Bad*, for example, chooses to become a meth producer upon learning that his disappointing life is going to end with a random case of lung cancer. The official explanation is that he wants to "provide for his family," although obviously his family would never have asked him to become a criminal and his wife (Anna Gunn) is horrified when she finds out. The deeper explanation becomes clear as the story unfolds: he has simply reached a breaking point and his diagnosis provides him with an excuse to assert himself after a lifetime of pathetic submission. These two explanations aren't contradictory, however, because "being a man"—being proud, making his own way in the world, answering to no one, etc.—is intimately tied up with "providing for his family." In fact, even after he has already made more money than his family could ever need and even after his wife has threatened him with divorce, a fellow criminal convinces him to stay in the game because "a man provides for his family." After watching *Breaking Bad* and hearing Bryan Cranston's continual evocations of *"this family,"* it is difficult for me to hear the word "family" without also hearing sinister overtones.

Far from undermining sociopathy, then, family ties often

prove to be the justification for sociopathic behavior. This is the case not only for the perpetrators, but for the family members who are its beneficiaries. Mafia stories, for instance, frequently feature women who are faced with a situation where their denial about their husband or father's behavior can no longer be maintained—but they almost always wind up coming around and making peace with their complicity. Even in *Breaking Bad*, Anna Gunn's character at first refuses to turn her husband in to the police and finally winds up involving herself in his business to make sure he doesn't get caught, all in the service of sparing the children the horror of learning their father is a criminal.

In short, family ties provide perfect rationalizations for the sociopaths and ease the transition into Stockholm Syndrome for the rest of the family. Family ties are thus, at least potentially, the most anti-social of social bonds—the traditional father, after all, views the wife and kids as essentially extensions of himself, so that caring for one's family can paradoxically be a profoundly selfish act. One can see this even in a show like *Weeds*, where a widow (Mary Louise Parker) fulfills the role of sociopathic father and starts dealing marijuana to provide for her family. Unlike in *Breaking Bad*, however, where the family really is pushed to the limit financially, the family in *Weeds* lives in a wealthy suburb, and the drug-dealing mother is motivated just as much by her desire to keep up appearances for the other women in town as by any real economic need. As in *Breaking Bad*, her family is initially upset when they learn of her unorthodox financial strategy but soon start helping her out, even as it becomes more and more clear that the drug-dealing parent enjoys the thrilling life of a criminal as an end in itself. The noble path of providing for their family, come what may, becomes indistinguishable from the choice to become a common criminal.

Even the apparently "redemptive" moment of the sociopath embracing family life thus confirms the sociopath's complete mastery—he can instrumentalize even the most natural and seemingly irresistible forms of social connection. The appeal of this fantasy is clear in a society that relies heavily on family ties as a means of blackmail, for instance in the US where a parent's need to keep a job in order to provide for the family is compounded by the link between employment and health insurance. Even more insidious is the ever-more-pervasive use of natural human sympathy, altruism, and desire for creative activity to exploit workers, enabling administrators to count on schoolteachers to buy extra school supplies themselves out of a desire to help their students, or to demand free labor in creative fields because they know people will "work for love" and do anything that might help them fulfill their dream of (eventually!) getting paid to do what they're passionate about.

The morality play that wants to present the sociopath's lack of social connection and morality as his greatest weakness thus serves as a compensation for the fact that the average person's natural sympathies and inclinations can truly be their greatest weakness in our decaying social order. In a broken society, it seems, only a broken person can succeed.

The varieties of sociopathic experience

I agree with the intuition that motivates the fantasy of the sociopath: our society really is broken. The question I would ask, however, is what we're using as a point of comparison. Every social norm, it seems, even the apparently "natural" social order of the family, can be exploited for sociopathic ends or be caught up in the vicious cycle that generates and supports sociopathic behavior. This is because, as I argued in *Awkwardness*, there is no "natural" social order—all social norms are no more than functional guidelines that we use to help us cope with the anxiety and conflict that comes with being the fundamentally social beings that we are. Rather than coming down from heaven or being grounded in some kind of natural law (such as the biological or evolutionary imperatives that supposedly ground the family structure), our social orders are long-term strategies for dealing with each other, tools that are useful in a given time and place with no guarantee that they will last.

The paradox is that it can be much more difficult to recognize those social tools as what they are when they are breaking down. It may be easier to rebel against a more stable social order, because the self-confidence that comes from a feeling of mastery over social interaction stays with us even as we fight against it— and the same may be true of the vague but ever-present anxiety that attends our state of cultural awkwardness. Threatened by the awkward abyss, we cling to our declining social norms and ask them to be more than they are or can be. We let them rule over us all the more as they fail to serve us, either by providing clear expectations or approximating some form of justice or fairness.

As courtship expectations become ever more unclear, for example, a young man or woman may become ever more convinced that there is a "right" thing to do in such matters, or at least a clear "wrong" thing to do (usually directly asking the person out on a date). As a result, they may wind up missing out on a good connection—something that happens frequently to the salesman Andy and the receptionist Erin in recent seasons of the US *Office*. Similarly, even as they watch less qualified workers get ahead, some people stick to the principle that it's rude to ask for a raise or promotion, or that it's even an offence that could get them fired. In sticking to principles they believe to be objective but that are in reality arbitrarily chosen, these timid individuals are getting the worst of both worlds: they don't get what they want, and they don't even get a genuine sense of fulfilling their social duty, as their belief that they're following some kind of social expectation is purely delusional.

In addition to pointing to the problem, then, the fantasy of the sociopath may be pointing toward a solution. If relating to social norms as tools is the mark of a sociopath, then perhaps we could all benefit from being more sociopathic. It may not be a matter of choosing between cynically manipulating social norms and faithfully following them, but of *choosing the goals* toward which we cynically manipulate them—meaning first of all that we need to abandon the path of manipulating them toward self-undermining ends. Indeed, the problem with fantasy sociopaths may be that they are not sociopathic enough, that their end goals wind up serving the system they have supposedly transcended and mastered.

Before getting to the possibility of a solution, however, I will need to outline the problem by tracing out the patterns and dynamics of the fantasy of the sociopath. Simply for the sake of navigating the truly massive set of examples, I will be limiting myself to characters from relatively recent television shows. I will move from "lower" to "higher" forms of sociopathy, seeking ultimately to ascend to a point where a sociopathic character may be transforming into something beyond a typical fantasy sociopath.

I will begin with the lowest form of TV sociopath, the point where sociopathy borders on psychopathy. These are characters that I call **schemers**. Examples include Homer Simpson, Peter Griffin of *Family Guy* (and cognate characters on its sister shows), Eric Cartman of *South Park*, the title character of *Archer*, and "The Gang" of *It's Always Sunny in Philadelphia*. All of these characters share the trait of scheming, and although they are uniformly self-seeking, their primary goals are either relative advantage (as when two characters in *Always Sunny* compete to be a third character's "best friend") or, most often, screwing someone over (as in Cartman's racially-motivated war against his Jewish friend Kyle). What threatens to cast these characters into the category of simple insanity is that their plans are often extremely short-sighted or deluded and their attention spans are often laughably short (as illustrated in the rapid-fire plot-twists of *The Simpsons*)—but their love of scheming and their fundamentally social goal of relative advantage or just "winning" an encounter push them into the realm of sociopathy, if only barely.

Building on this zero-degree of sociopathy, I will move onto a class of more rational schemers, whom I call the **climbers**. These sociopaths use their skills at seduction and manipulation to get ahead, usually in very clearly-defined ways. Many examples of this class can be found in "reality television," particularly those like *Big Brother* or *Survivor* that amount to long-running game shows. The sociopathy of the contestants is such a well-established theme that there are now annual YouTube compilations of reality-show participants proclaiming, "I'm not here to make friends!" Even in more free-form reality shows, however, there is an element of climbing due to the chance of becoming a kind of free-floating cultural icon. Snookie of *Jersey Shore* and Sarah Palin of the 2008 U.S. Presidential Election are good examples of the latter phenomenon.

Climbers are also well-represented in scripted drama, particularly in teen dramas such as *Gossip Girl* or *Glee*. Among "highbrow" shows, there is Don Draper of *Mad Men*, in many ways the best example of the contemporary sociopath, who abandons his rural, lower-class roots by stealing the identity of a fellow soldier, then climbs relentlessly to the top of the advertising profession. Similarly, Stringer Bell of *The Wire* tries and fails to escape from the confines of gang life by leveraging his drug wealth to become a legitimate property developer. Though both characters are in a very real sense self-made men, the paradox of their stories is that while they succeed to some degree in escaping from the constraints of their immediate social settings, they can only do so by following the impersonal dictates of social expectations.

In the climber category, one might also place other gang leaders such as Tony Soprano or *Deadwood*'s Al Swearingen — though Swearingen might also belong to the next, more "noble" category of sociopaths, the **enforcers**. Many of these characters are literally in some form of law enforcement, such as *The Wire*'s McNulty, *24*'s Jack Bauer, the rogue police unit in *The Shield*, Kyra Sedgwick's character on *The Closer*, or the cowboy-style lawman of *Justified*. They are sociopathically devoted to their jobs—following the common trope of police dramas, their work weakens their faith in humanity but is nonetheless profoundly addictive—and yet this leads them to continually violate the law. Jack Bauer, for instance, is famously willing to use torture to prevent terrorist attacks, and McNulty at one point responds to budget cuts by creating a fake serial killer and redirecting the unlimited funding to other investigations. One can also see this phenomenon outside of law enforcement, as in the cases of Dexter or House, yet the rogue police officer remains very much the model. In all these cases, the violation of the law is committed for the sake of the law, to achieve the goals that the law cannot achieve when enforced literally. These characters represent the ultimate "necessary evil," whose anti-social tendencies keep the social order from collapsing.

The path of my analysis, then, will move from the bottom-feeding schemer to the self-seeking climber and all the way up to the self-sacrificing enforcer—and perhaps also beyond, to an even more radically sociopathic form of sociopathy. In conclusion, I will ask what all of these characters may be able to teach us about how to actualize the hope at the heart of our sociopathic fantasies: the hope that we, too, might have sociopathy, and have it more abundantly.

Chapter 1

The Schemers

In a two-part episode of *South Park*, the show's star, Eric Cartman, joins forces with Bart Simpson against a common enemy: their new-found competitor in the realm of irreverent, adult-oriented cartoon shows, *Family Guy*. After a brief debate over which child is more of a trouble-maker and should thus take the lead, Cartman triumphs when he reveals that he once fed chili made from the flesh of a classmate's own parents to him for revenge. What's so remarkable about this incident is that Cartman's cannibalistic chili isn't the only trump card he could've used against Bart. This fourth grader has had a remarkable career in mayhem. One episode has him stumbling across dead fetuses, which inspires him to start his own business selling fetuses for their stem cells. In another, he starts a wildly successful Christian band on a bet, substituting the name "Jesus" into popular love songs and writing similarly-themed originals (such as "I Want to Get Down on My Knees and Start Pleasing Jesus"), and then, finding that the Christian music industry gives out Myrrh Albums instead of the Gold Album necessary to win his bet, Cartman exclaims to a horrified audience of Christians: "Fuck Jesus!" Yet another finds him somehow installed as a teacher of at-risk urban youth and serving as an inspirational teacher like Jaime Escalante of the film *Stand and Deliver*—except that Cartman teaches them cheating (the white person's path to success!) instead of calculus.

Even when he's not engaged in large-scale evil plots, Cartman is personally abrasive. Based on the classic TV character Archie Bunker, he indulges in every possible form of bigotry. He is sexist, as when he laughs at the idea of breast cancer, asking to be shown these fantastical "killer boobies." He is racist, persistently referring to the one black student in his class (subtly named Token) as "you black asshole." Above all, however, he is anti-Semitic, leading him to continually torment and distrust his Jewish friend Kyle—and in one episode, inspired by a viewing of Mel Gibson's *Passion of the Christ*, he goes so far as to dress like Hitler and incite the members of a *Passion* fan club to attempt a reprise of the Final Solution. He is also homophobic and classist, as illustrated by an anti-gay on-camera rant during an episode where he is acting like a stupid redneck in the hopes of thereby succeeding as a NASCAR driver.

On top of his malice and prejudice, Cartman is whiny, pushy, and selfish. His voice is annoying and harsh and, in what is normally the kiss of death for one's playground popularity, he is extremely obese. He is, in short, presented as the most loathsome possible character on every level, and most of his classmates, including even his nominal "best friends," hate him. At the same time, Cartman is too evil to be satisfied with plots that he can pull off single-handed—and more often than not, he winds up with more than enough followers. These followers can be total strangers, as when he leads a group of Civil War reenactors to reopen hostilities, pushing back Union forces so decisively that President Clinton formally surrenders. Yet they can also be those who know him best, such as his three primary co-stars, Kyle (whom he constantly insults for being Jewish), Kenny (whom he continually torments for being poor), and Stan (of whom he is jealous for his relative popularity), or in later episodes, his long-suffering sidekick, the pathetic Butters.

Given the fact that large crowds are uniformly presented as idiotic in *South Park*, perhaps Cartman's success in misleading them is understandable—but what are we to make of his manipulation of those who ought to know better? What is it about this repulsive schemer that is so seductive, not only to his fellow cartoon characters but also to the show's audience and even its own creators? Trey Parker and Matt Stone, the duo behind *South Park*, reportedly based the characters of Stan and Kyle on themselves, yet have frequently said that Cartman is their favorite, an assessment shared by most fans. What accounts for the widespread fascination with this foul-mouthed child?

In order to answer this question, I believe it is helpful to situate *South Park* within the broader genre that the opening scene of this chapter highlights: the adult-oriented cartoon. That means first of all relating *South Park* to its predecessor, *The Simpsons*, the founder of the adult cartoon genre, and in particular relating Cartman to Bart Simpson. Why has Cartman become so central to *South Park* while Bart has been replaced by his father, Homer, as the central character of *The Simpsons*? What is Cartman delivering, what fantasy is he fulfilling, and why has Bart failed by comparison?

The decline of the lovable scamp

When I was a child, I wasn't allowed to watch *The Simpsons*. To some extent, this was understandable: my parents were fairly conservative, and Fox was associated with some pretty raunchy and racy material at the time, perhaps most notably the sitcom *Married...With Children*. Yet when I watch the early episodes, it's hard for me to see what they really would have objected to in the show had they watched it themselves. Bart is certainly a trouble-maker, and the low-class setting of the show perhaps lent itself to crass behaviors that my parents would disapprove of. Overall, however, Bart's escapades were arguably less subversive than the sheer mayhem one would find in the average episode of *Dennis the Menace*. In fact, compared to the latter character, Bart is simply boring. He is unintelligent and certainly not nearly as clever as Dennis the Menace, and he consistently lacks the courage of his convictions with regard to his troublemaking, often regretting his mischief or even trying to stop plots that he has put in motion.

The t-shirts might have proclaimed that Bart was a proud underachiever, but the plots of most of the episodes showed him to be essentially a normal—even a mediocre—kid. There is certainly something to be said for an honest portrayal of childhood, and the early episodes that focused on the struggles of Bart's more sensitive and intellectually curious sister, Lisa, remain fan favorites to this day. Yet unflinching honesty seems an unlikely path to becoming the longest-running primetime program on American television, as *The Simpsons* became in 2009. (The more likely outcome for a show characterized by its honesty, such as the high school drama *My So-Called Life*, is critical acclaim, a devoted cult following, cancellation after a season or two, and steady DVD sales driven by word of mouth recommendations of the "underappreciated gem.")

Furthermore, a more or less straightforward presentation of *anything* feels particularly inappropriate for a cartoon. Like many children, I know that I strongly preferred cartoons and found most live-action programs boring, for the simple reason that in a cartoon, anything can happen. A boring old car can transform into a robot! Huge anthropomorphic turtles can learn the martial arts and fight crime! Rabbits can fight back against their hunters (often in drag)! Live action shows frequently have the same fantasy element, but it's the core competency of animation, which more than live action directly actualizes the wonder of television and film: the wonder of a picture coming to life. *The Simpsons'* predecessors in the animated sitcom genre, *The Flintstones* and *The Jetsons*, had the fantasy element built-in, and a large part of their humor came from trying to reproduce everyday modern life in a much different setting, as in the use of dinosaurs for appliances or the sentient robot maid. We can see a present-day kid getting in trouble and maybe learning moral lessons anywhere— using a cartoon to deliver that familiar product seems like a waste.

Over time, the writers of *The Simpsons* seemed to realize the limitations of using Bart as a central character and, in what would become a defining moment for the adult cartoon genre, gradually shifted their attention to Bart's father, Homer. A selfish, ignorant, and lazy man given to alcohol abuse as well as child abuse (the iconic "why you little..." followed by strangulation), Homer initially seems an unlikely hero. This is not only due to lack of sympathy but due to his seeming lack of competence to do much other than perform poorly at his job, slink away to the bar, and consistently disappoint his wife and children. In principle, Homer should be as boring as Bart, but the twist the writers introduced was to make the dad into the Dennis the Menace character, who makes up for his lack of competence through the greater power that comes from being an adult—for instance, having money, being able to drive, and commanding at least some token respect and deference from his fellow adults.

This was the fantasy that made *The Simpsons* such an enduring fixture: the fantasy of a child who not only has the body of an adult (this phenomenon is all too familiar), but can *act on* his childish motivations without suffering the consequences. He has all the benefits of being an adult—including a long-suffering wife to clean up after him—but is not bound by any of the responsibilities, because he is, after all, a cartoon character. He can crash the car, or go to work drunk, or burn down the house, or alienate the entire town, or get entangled with the mafia, or whatever other bizarre scenario the writers dream up, and next week everything will be back to square one.

Taking it a step further, Homer is perhaps even more a child than children themselves, as his adult status frees him from any effective restraint, such as that of parents, teachers, or other authority figures short of the police. This enables him to act on his every impulse, and the lack of any "reality principle" allows his reasoning—if that is what it should be called—to become ever more random and unpredictable. For example, one episode begins with a bizarre non-sequitur that leads Homer to jump from making advance funeral arrangements for his father to installing a tennis court in his backyard—and once it's installed, he's exclaims, "*This* is tennis?!," as he apparently thought a "tennis court" was the name for a "foxy boxing" arena where attractive women would engage in hand-to-hand combat. Yet he quickly recovers from his disappointment, embarking on an adventure that ultimately puts him in contact with many of the best tennis stars in the world. By the next episode, of course, the tennis court is gone and the entire affair has been forgotten.

Homer's central status in *The Simpsons* was well-established by the time *South Park* debuted in 1997. This was a show that took the notion of an adult-oriented cartoon seriously, taking advantage of the looser restraints of a cable (as opposed to broadcast) network to fill the show with raunchy, irreverent, and crude content as well as the fantasy elements the cartoons do best. For instance, the very first episode features Cartman receiving an alien "anal probe" that periodically reemerges and expands to the size of a small building, and the show mocks the convention of resetting everything to normal each episode by killing off the same character, Kenny, every single episode for the first five seasons (and many episodes since). Yet the show has remained resolutely focused on child characters, never shifting the primary focus to any of the adults.

What accounts for this difference? I believe that *South Park* managed to maintain its focus on child characters by enacting the same basic fantasy that Homer Simpson fulfills, except in the opposite direction. That is to say, Cartman represents an adult in a child's body. The show's creators have often claimed that Cartman is based on the sitcom character Archie Bunker, whose narrow-minded views contemporary audiences would never tolerate coming from an adult character—they can only be expressed if put in the mouth of a child.

Along with these "adult" opinions that seem to have come from nowhere (his mother certainly demonstrates no biases), the writers also give him a variety of other adult-like qualities, most notably focus, concentration, and the ability to create long-term plans. Where Homer drifts aimlessly from impulse to impulse, Cartman seeks his goals with an often obsessive focus. Yet Cartman's goals remain, for the most part, those of a child. For instance, one multi-episode series opens with Cartman waiting impatiently for the Nintendo Wii's release date, which is two weeks away—in the eyes of a child, a veritable lifetime. Unable to bear the waiting, he arranges for his hapless friend Butters to "cryogenically freeze" him (by burying him in the snow) and then unfreeze him when the two weeks are up. He winds up being buried by an avalanche and only unfrozen many centuries later, but despite being in a futuristic environment filled with marvels (including highly evolved sea otters that are making war with humans), he maintains his megalomaniacal focus on the Nintendo Wii, ultimately devising a scheme to travel back in time when it becomes clear that the video game system is no longer available in the future.

In another episode, he imprisons Butters in a fallout shelter for two weeks and convinces him a nuclear strike has occurred, all so that he can be invited in Butters' place to a birthday party at a Mexican restaurant called Casa Mamita, which includes rides and other gimmicky attractions. Butters finds his way home on the day of the party, however, and police are there to intercept Cartman when he arrives at the restaurant—yet he runs past them and quickly visits all the tacky attractions, ultimately surrendering to police with all the serenity of a boy whose deepest desires have been fulfilled.

Even more important than any fleeting pleasure is Cartman's desire to one-up his friends, particularly his Jewish friend Kyle. Here again he displays amazing resourcefulness and focus. In the episode where he's trying to get *Family Guy* cancelled, a significant part of his motivation is the fact that Kyle likes the show, and he makes a cross-country voyage on his "big wheel" tricycle to sabotage Kyle's attempt to save it. Another multi-part episode focuses on Cartman's attempt to make good on Kyle's claim that Kyle would "suck his balls" if Cartman could show him a real leprechaun. When Kyle does in fact see the leprechaun, he refuses to comply—and Cartman ultimately takes his case all the way to the Supreme Court, which orders Kyle to fulfill his promise.

What all this shows is that Cartman isn't fully self-aware in the sense of literally being an adult stuck in a child's body—a condition that actually sounds terrifying to me. Cartman can't recognize his childish desires as petty and pointless, for instance, and just as Homer is more impulsive than any actual child as a result of his adult status, so also is Cartman even more childish in his desires than any actual child as a result of his adult competence. There is a level, however, on which Cartman *does* seem to be very aware that he's a child, and that is in recognizing how much a child can really get away with.

One of the things that allows human society to function is that children don't realize how powerful they are. I have often wished that my parents hadn't made me participate in certain things—for instance, I hated going to summer camp. Yet when I think about it, how exactly were they "making" me go? If I was absolutely dedicated to avoiding summer camp, were they going to tie me up and throw me into the car? Even if so, what would keep me from trying to escape? The same goes for many things that children experience as an imposition: in reality, the only thing "making" them go is their instinctive obedience to their parents, an obedience that is certainly based in love, but that is reinforced by the feelings of guilt and shame that most often accompany disobedience.

Cartman lacks all of that. His absolute commitment to his goals leads him to continually and mercilessly badger his mother, who is amazingly passive in the face of her obnoxious and demanding son and nearly always gives him what he wants.

Where Homer is perhaps more psychopathic than strictly socio-pathic, Cartman is completely sociopathic in his lack of empathy, to the point where he doesn't seem to love even his own mother—indeed, doesn't seem to understand the very concept of love. And just as the fantasy of TV sociopathy dictates, that very lack of empathy is what makes him so ruthlessly effective in achieving his ridiculous and meaningless goals.

Turning the tables, Cartman routinely gives his own mother a guilt trip, often inducing her to aid him in even his most insane plans—such as his desire to fake a mental disability and partic-ipate in the Special Olympics, as he reasons that he would surely be able to win easily against the handicapped—and more broadly provide him with the kind of resources that a child generally lacks. On the rare occasions when she fights back, he simply doubles down on his guilt tripping, in one case going so far as to publicly accuse her of "fucking him" by not giving him what he wants—a plotline that culminates with her being casti-gated as a child molester on national television.

Enabling mothers, MILFs, and negative feminism

Cartman's mom isn't always a failure as a parent, however. There is one episode where she effectively resists him, hiring the Dog Whisperer to train her disobedient son. After much resistance, Cartman eventually submits to the training regime and becomes an upstanding young boy who does his homework and chores without being asked and seeks permission for even the smallest indulgence. The message here seems clear: mom was to blame for Cartman's behavior, and as soon as she takes responsibility for the situation, he straightens up. At the end of the episode, however, the writers throw in an additional twist—Cartman's single mom, who is frequently portrayed as a prostitute, a porn actress, and generally promiscuous, reveals that she was only cooperating with the training regime because she hoped to start a relationship with the Dog Whisperer. When he says that he saw her as just another client, she returns home and begins indulging Cartman again, ensuring a return to his old ways.

South Park isn't known for its progressive social views, so perhaps one could write off this misogynistic plotline as a bit of "provocative" anti-feminism. Yet this link between sociopathic man-child combinations and mothers who are both indulgent and strangely sexualized is common in the adult cartoon genre. Marge Simpson, for instance, arguably serves more as a kind of indulgent mother to Homer than as a wife—but the two have one of the healthiest sex lives of any married couple in the history of TV, to the point where one suspects that Marge's tolerance of Homer's antics is tied directly to his performance in the bedroom. Viewed in this light, Cartman's mom is a variation on the theme, indulging her son's behavior because he serves as a kind of substitute for the meaningful adult relationship she seems unable to achieve.

It all seems like a bizarre twist on Freud's Oedipus complex. Freud famously claimed that male children's desire to possess their mother led them to want to kill their father (as rival for mother's affections) and that induction into human society meant accepting the prohibition of incest and identifying with the father (as representative of impersonal cultural authority), ultimately finding another woman to make up for the loss of the mother. Both Cartman and Homer, however, manage to possess their (literal or only slightly figurative) mothers, and this seems directly tied to their freedom from the social norms that go along with identifying with the father. The fact that Cartman's induction into normal social life corresponds with his mother's belief that she has found a potential husband only reinforces this connection.

The same basic pattern can be found in Seth MacFarlane's *Family Guy*, which is a kind of synthesis of *The Simpsons* and *South Park*. The show features both a Homer-like sociopathic father (Peter) and a Cartman-like adult in a child's body, in this case a baby who can talk and has considerable adult knowledge (Stewie). Yet not content with imitating existing forms, *Family Guy* adds in an adult in a *dog's* body as well (Brian). As in both previous shows, the mother (Lois) is strongly sexualized—everyone in town, including their dog Brian, wants to sleep with her, and she and Peter enjoy sex with a Simpson-esque enthusiasm.

Yet both the adult-child characters go a step beyond their predecessors in their relationship with the mother figure. Peter, for one, is much more clearly sociopathic than Homer, who is still vulnerable to guilt trips from Marge and Lisa. His lack of any empathy or indeed any recognizably human emotion is so total that he can go further than Homer's thoughtlessness and be actively abusive toward his wife. Meanwhile, Stewie, himself a strangely sexualized baby who embodies Freud's "polymorphous perversity" in his curiosity about every kind of sexual fetish, frequently seeks to murder Lois, particularly in the early seasons. The reason for his hostility is no more clearly explained than is his easy access to science-fiction weaponry such as death rays—just as with his younger age, his outright hatred of his mother appears to be simply a way to do his predecessor one better.

All this is a little difficult to take—indeed, Peter may be one of the most obnoxious characters in the history of television, sometimes rendering *Family Guy* almost unwatchable. As if acknowledging this problem, both of Seth MacFarlane's spin-off shows, *American Dad* and *The Cleveland Show*, dial things back to a more *Simpsons*-like level. Both get rid of the malicious and sexualized baby, for instance, replacing Stewie with a polymorphously perverse alien named Roger (in *American Dad*) and with a baby whose appeal is simply the fact that he talks (in *The Cleveland Show*). Both husbands are irrational and unreliable like Homer, both wives are more or less long-suffering like Marge, and both shows frequently feature the kinds of sympathetic reconciliation scenes that are so typical of sitcoms in general.

Yet I believe that *Family Guy*'s extreme revisions of the conventions laid out by *The Simpsons* and *South Park* reveal the underlying sexism that these shows carry over from the traditional sitcoms they satirize. Marge's love for Homer is a variation on the common combination of "dumpy guy" and "hot wife" in live-action sitcoms—beyond her superhuman loyalty, her initial attraction to this fat, stupid man is far from plausible. A similar pattern can be seen in the young girls of the shows. The girls of *South Park* are all more or less "normal" and featureless, dutiful students who occasionally become boy crazy, while Lisa Simpson is amazingly responsible and a virtual genius compared to the rest of the town.

Just as in the films of Judd Apatow, a body of work that appeals to much the same audience as adult cartoons, women basically represent responsibility and adulthood—or at least they do when they don't represent effortless wish fulfillment. Female characters almost never get to participate in the scheming fun of the males, and when they hatch schemes of their own, it is often played off as pathetic or creepy. Meg, the daughter from *Family Guy*, is a particularly vivid example. Though she is by all appearances an average teenage girl in every way, Peter and the rest of the family inexplicably single her out for abuse, frequently referring to her as ugly. On the rare occasion when she gets her own plotline, it normally revolves around a creepy attachment to a male figure who shows her some minimal kindness—including, at one point, Brian the dog. Other unattached women in these shows are portrayed in a similarly negative light, most notably the subtly named teacher Ms. Choksondik of *South Park*, who is portrayed with repulsively long breasts that swing wildly every time she moves. In a world where the mother and the sex object are combined, it appears that the only role available for women who aren't sexually available (like a sister or a teacher) is that of the repulsive hag.

One partial exception to this rule is the recent adult cartoon *Archer*, which injects an adult cartoon ethos into the world of 1960s spy comic books, which are the inspiration for its unique animation style. The main character is Sterling Archer, an international spy working for the ISIS agency that is run by his domineering mother, Mallory Archer. Sterling replaces the suave coolness of James Bond with the wonder of a child who is continually impressed by his own "awesome" exploits, hence constituting a kind of variation on Homer Simpson. The major innovation from the standpoint of the present analysis, however, is the replacement of the endlessly accommodating mother with an uncaring mother who—wonder of wonders!—often has her own agenda to pursue. The two have a bizarre Oedipal relationship that keeps Sterling from forming an adult relationship—he is frequently portrayed answering his mother's trivial phone calls in the middle of sex, for instance—and of course the existence of her agency is what allows Sterling to pull off his adventures, yet the two are fundamentally equals and often rivals.

Freeing the mother from her purely instrumental role seems to have created room for other female characters to exercise autonomy as well, most notably Sterling's fellow agent and former lover Lana. Though Lana pays lip service to the stereotype that women are more responsible, she is often just as self-indulgent as Sterling, particularly during the frequent episodes when the two engage in the kind of petty one-upmanship normally seen only between young boys on these shows.

The show does include plenty of misogynistic content, revolving around Sterling's childish instrumentalization of sex as yet one more "awesome" exploit. Yet the women characters—most notably Mallory and Lana—instrumentalize sex just as much, and Sterling's mistreated partners often find a way to screw him over as revenge. Sterling's mistreatment of women thus must be placed into the broader context of the show's toxic nihilism and misanthropy, traits to which, again, women and men appear to have equal access in the show's universe.

Thus, in what is surely a triumph of feminism, *Archer* shows that women, too, can be childish schemers. This twisted principle of gender equality seems to me to result directly from the inclusion of the mother within the field of scheming, which means granting the mother (the archetypal woman) independent agency and thus removing her from the passive and enabling role of the mother found in *The Simpsons*, *South Park*, and *Family Guy*. Sterling's butler, Woodhouse, who effectively raised him while Mallory was cutting her teeth as a spy, does serve as a kind of surrogate mother and receives his fair share of abuse and mistreatment—yet Woodhouse is almost impossibly elderly and frail, a kind of living embodiment of the withering away of the traditional motherly role as the necessary condition for the fantasy of the adult child. While this particular fantasy found its initial ground in the dynamics of the "traditional" family, it is increasingly leaving behind those roots and taking on a life of its own.

A show about nihilism

If the central fantasy of the adult cartoon show is the overlap and coincidence of adult and child, then I propose that some live-action comedies are essentially live-action cartoons. One that springs immediately to mind is *Married...With Children*, whose down-and-out father, Al Bundy, arguably laid the groundwork for the development of Homer Simpson—and whose cartoon-ishly busty mother figure, Peg, certainly corresponds to the enduring archetype of the long-suffering and sexualized mother of the adult cartoon show. Yet I'd like to focus more on shows that, like *Archer*, move past the family dynamic and allow room for women to be schemers, too. In particular, I'd like to look at a show that I regard as instrumental in mainstreaming this fantasy of the scheming sociopath, namely *Seinfeld*.

Seinfeld is famously a "show about nothing." The show follows the adventures of comedian Jerry, his best friend George, his ex-girlfriend Elaine, and his insane neighbor Kramer as they deal with everyday conflicts and annoyances in New York City. Many have focused on the "observational humor" of the show and its attendant ironic detachment, as even the most mundane and unquestioned aspects of life become fodder for bemused remarks along the lines of "what's the deal with belts? I mean, *come on!*"

Equally important to the show's appeal, however, are the elaborate schemes the characters regularly come up with—schemes that, unlike the characters' meaningless everyday lives, engage them very passionately, at least for the span of an episode. To take one memorable example, George gets a high score on the arcade game *Frogger* and purchases the machine to preserve his record. He then discovers that he must leave the machine plugged in or else erase its memory, and so he devotes prodigious efforts to transporting it while leaving it plugged in, only to see the machine destroyed as he tries to imitate the titular frog in weaving his way across a busy street.

Everything about this plot is childish: the pride in video game skills (notably an antique video game George might have played as a teenager), the outlandish attempt to preserve an essentially meaningless honor, and the concluding attempt to imitate a video game in real life. A close look at a wide range of classic *Seinfeld* plots reveals their essentially childish nature. There is petty one-upsmanship, as in the famous "contest" to see who can abstain from masturbation the longest—a contest in which Elaine notably participates and quickly gives up. Indeed, sexuality is a domain of profound childishness for all involved, as when Kramer goes on a quest to impregnate a woman just to prove he can, or George tries to combine eating and sex, or more generally Jerry and Elaine break up with partner after partner with all the arbitrarity of a child refusing to eat a sandwich that hasn't been cut diagonally.

George's devotion to his *Frogger* score stands in stark contrast to his reluctant engagement, which ends when his fiancée dies from licking the poisonous envelopes he purchased for their wedding invitations—an event that meets with a shrug. Similarly, an episode where Jerry has convinced himself that Elaine is actually the love of his life and he must marry her before she gets away sees Jerry shrugging off the plan completely once he grows tired of the idea. The difference here is clear: any plan that results in leading a normal adult life quickly falls by the wayside, while childish plots are pushed to the absolute limit.

A major contribution to this lack of any real inhibition is the fact that *Seinfeld* breaks with long-standing tradition by making the main female character, Elaine, neither a mother nor a potential love interest. As Jerry's ex-girlfriend, she is for all practical purposes sexually unavailable to Jerry—with the exception of one episode where they have sex one last time to prove that Jerry can bring her to orgasm and thereby "save the friendship," an attempt that fails without doing any apparent damage to their relationship—and, due to the typical honor code of young men, unavailable to his friends as well. With the potential for sex eliminated, Jerry and the other men have no reason to be on their best behavior in front of her. At the same time, her active sex life disqualifies her as a mother figure and further emphasizes the fact that she is simply a peer, perhaps even "one of the guys."

Of course, what enables their behavior on a practical level is the fact that, at least for most of the show's run, most of the characters (other than the enigmatic Kramer) have gainful employment of the kind that allows for plenty of free time. This baseline competence in life shows through in other respects, as most of the characters show some basic understanding of what kind of behavior is acceptable, as well as the intelligence needed to endlessly analyze those very social norms. The lack of any family responsibilities—along with their cynicism and basic lack of empathy—allows them to indulge themselves in childish pursuits, but with adult resources. Clearly this is a variation on the fantasy of Homer, and in fact it is a fantasy that, for all the subversiveness of *Seinfeld*, matches up pretty closely with the aspirations of many young urbanites in the 1990s and 2000s alike. After such a long run, the infamous finale where the fantasy bubble is punctured and the characters receive the comeuppance for their sociopathic behavior was too little, too late.

The toehold in reality that *Seinfeld* tried to maintain is completely lost in the show that I believe is a new *Seinfeld* for our contemporary reality: *It's Always Sunny in Philadelphia*, which debuted in 2005. A key mutation of *Seinfeld* comes from the primary setting. Where *Seinfeld* took place primarily in Jerry's apartment or a nearby diner, the main setting for *Always Sunny* collapses the two together: it is a bar (hence public like the diner) that they all own together (hence private like the apartment). Yet the characters show no aptitude whatsoever for running a bar and it is in fact remarkably unsuccessful—except for a couple episodes where they devise some scheme to boost revenues for a short period, their only customers appear to be two homeless men, who pour themselves free beers during the long periods when none of the main characters are actually present at the bar. Hence the characters' "job," such as it is, is not a connection to the world of adult competence at all, but is instead a previous scheme that is now persisting out of sheer inertia. In other words, their life is a scheme *all the way down*.

In addition, in its first season, it had an ensemble cast that was remarkably similar in structure to the *Seinfeld* cast: two more or less "normal" guys (Dennis and Mack, one of whom is more "successful" while the other is more pathetic), one woman connected to one of the normal guys (Dee, this time Dennis's sister rather than his ex-girlfriend), and one crazy guy (Charlie).

Unlike in *Seinfeld*, where only Jerry and George were childhood friends, in *Always Sunny*, all four characters have known each other since they were kids, a connection that is reinforced by the shift from an ex-girlfriend to a sister for the primary female character. In its second season, the characters' childishness is further emphasized as Dennis and Dee's father Frank (played by Danny DeVito) comes on the scene and asks to join "The Gang" as a way of escaping adult responsibilities.

Where *Seinfeld* simply excluded the role of the idealized-sexualized mother, *Always Sunny*, like *Archer*, mutates and displaces it. Dennis and Dee's mother is portrayed as promiscuous—for instance, she once sleeps with Mack, who becomes smitten with her, and it is revealed that Dennis and Dee are actually the products of an affair—but she is also cold and scheming, similar to Mallory Archer. And far from being central to the plot, she is soon unceremoniously killed off. Frank becomes a replacement "mother" in terms of accommodating The Gang's schemes due to his fabulous wealth (itself gained through a lifetime of adult scheming), but after it is revealed that he isn't Dennis and Dee's biological father, he becomes, much more even than Mallory Archer, simply another member of the group. As expected, then, while the members of The Gang tend to evince the "no girls allowed" attitude typical of cliques of young boys, Dee schemes with the best of them, indeed often more destructively—as when she convinces a high school friend who had a crush on her to leave the priesthood in order to marry her, only to grow bored of the idea and back out. As a result, he becomes a homeless drug addict.

Frank's wealth and the lack of any concrete adult responsibilities aside from their failed bar means that, like Homer, the *Always Sunny* characters lack any "reality principle." More than the *Seinfeld* characters, then, they live in "their own little world," displaying increasingly warped reasoning in their conversations and schemes. Dennis and Dee, for instance, spend one episode collecting unemployment and decide that they enjoy it so much that they want to go on welfare. Yet, reasoning that people on welfare are all crack addicts, they decide to start using crack so that they'll be prepared for the application process. Charlie stands out here for sheer insanity—perhaps as a result of sniffing glue and huffing paint, Charlie often appears to be genuinely mentally ill. He lacks any common sense and even common knowledge, in many episodes demonstrating his illiteracy and even an inability to tell his left from his right. He lives in abject squalor in an apartment with no bathroom (which he later winds up sharing with Frank), regularly eats garbage, and is said to have traded most of his shares in the bar for half of an old sandwich. Many of his plots center around winning the affections of a character known only as The Waitress (the actor's real-life wife), and his methods include pretending to have cancer so as to win her sympathy and writing a musical in which he will "reveal" his love for her.

Perhaps the most purely sociopathic character, however, is Dennis, whose wealthy upbringing and relative good looks give him a truly impressive sense of entitlement. His focus is on the apparently "adult" goal of seducing women, and one episode is centered on his method of emotional manipulation, which he proudly calls "The D.E.N.N.I.S. System." The guys are all eager to learn this system, while Dee is appalled and points out that he has developed an elaborate means to basically have sex with a woman a handful of times and then permanently alienate her. Yet Dennis's joy in recounting his methods shows that manipulation is, for him, an end in itself—and here Dennis is representative of The Gang in general, who frequently come up with a scheme just for the sake of something to do. One episode even makes this explicit as it follows several abortive attempts to come up with a scheme to keep themselves occupied. Even more than the bar, then, the very act of coming up with schemes is the overarching scheme within which this show takes place.

Childish games: Adult edition

In their scheming-for-scheming's-sake, these childish TV sociopaths are responding to the central problem of childhood, at least for the more privileged segments of Western society: *boredom*. At school and home alike, children are constantly struggling to find some way around this terrible affliction, to find something, *anything*, to *do!* Another common feature of these adult cartoon shows, whether animated or live-action, comes at this same problem from another direction: in nearly every episode, the scheme ends at least poorly, and often very destructively. Cartman almost always suffers terribly as a result of his malevolent schemes, and the other characters either receive their comeuppance or cause someone else some terrible harm—or both.

In *South Park*, these persistent failures are framed within a self-mocking moralism, signaled by the repeated formula, "You see, I've learned something today...." Yet there seems to me to be a deeper necessity at work in these constant failures. These childish schemes simply *cannot* work, precisely because they are the schemes of a child. A child is always threatened by the lack of anything to do because a child, as a child, can't really do *anything*. That is to say, a child can't really achieve anything with enduring meaning. These children with adult powers can "do whatever they want" only because for them, nothing really counts. From an adult perspective, this can represent a kind of intoxicating freedom, but within the child's frame, it can feel like a prison.

To really achieve something, one must unfortunately grow up—and that is what the sociopathic climbers I will discuss next chapter want to do above all. Before turning to this more mature brand of sociopath, however, I would like to look at one last show that seems to me to fall into the category of a live-action cartoon: *30 Rock*. A show that takes us behind the scenes of a second-tier sketch comedy show, it features Tina Fey as Liz Lemon, the head writer who must struggle to keep her stars and writers in line

while currying the favor of corporate management, here represented by Alec Baldwin's Jack Donaghy.

30 Rock represents a rarity in television, a comedy show with
a pathetic and incompetent *female* lead. Like *Archer*, it practices a
kind of negative feminism, showing that men and women are
both equally capable of petty scheming. What is particularly
interesting from my perspective, however, is how often the petty
schemes closely correspond to adult goals. The single Liz Lemon,
for instance, goes through a brief period of trying to adopt a
child, seemingly just for something to do—and the plotline is
unceremoniously dropped. A co-star of the sketch show, Jenna
Moroni, is continually engaged in petty one-upmanship, yet her
one-upmanship is an attempt to maintain her celebrity status
and acting career. Another of the sketch show's stars, Tracy
Jordan, suddenly gets it in his head to "EGOT," that is, to win an
Emmy, Grammy, Oscar, and Tony, a plot that replaces his equally
capricious desire to have a daughter. All of these are ostensibly
worthwhile adult achievements, yet they are pursued with all
the arbitrary and fickleness of a child.

Perhaps most subversive is the inclusion of Jack, an upwardly
mobile corporate executive, as just one character among others in
this childish milieu. On the one hand, his adult achievements
and power are routinely exaggerated, as though they're being
seen through a child's eyes—for instance, he frequently "slips"
and reveals that he's part of a Republican conspiracy to
undermine Obama, and his references to the privileges of great
wealth take on cartoonish dimensions, as when he raves about a
restaurant that, in place of a lobster tank, has a "veal tank,"
where "you can choose your own." On the other hand, his
striving for corporate power is portrayed as childish in a variety
of ways. He takes petty snipes at his corporate rivals, hatching
improbable plots to discredit them with the same gusto and
illogic of Cartman trying to undermine Kyle, while from the
other direction his devotion to his initial corporate mentor is

similar to the idealization of a father by his son.

Later in the series, when he gets a new corporate overlord, his long-term plot to take over the company requires him to compete with someone who is literally a child: the CEO's young grand-daughter, whom he tries to manipulate into choosing a non-corporate career so that she will be uninterested in running the company when she comes of age. When he tries to cultivate her interest in marine biology, he finds himself entranced by what was once his own boyhood passion and even briefly considers ditching the corporate life to follow his long-repressed dream. Fittingly, at the end of the episode, it is revealed that the grand-daughter was aware of his plot the whole time. She only pretended to enjoy marine biology, precisely because she had learned that it was an obsession of Jack and hoped to lure *him* from the corporate track and thereby eliminate him as a rival.

At the outer limits of the scheming adult cartoon genre, then, *30 Rock* undermines the very terms of the fantasy of the adult child. Where the other shows demonstrate again and again that it ultimately sucks to be a child because no adult accomplishment is possible, *30 Rock* undermines the fantasy from the other direction by asking whether even adults can truly be "adults" in any meaningful sense. In this respect, one of the greatest classics of Western literature anticipates this cartoonish sitcom. Writing in the late fifth century from the outskirts of a declining empire, St. Augustine, in his *Confessions*, tackles the same problem while assessing his own upbringing, castigating the hypocrisy of his parents and teachers who disciplined him for indulging in childish games, even while training him to advance in life by participating in adult games (in his day focused on rhetorical rather than financial manipulation) that were just as meaningless, but much more harmful—and, as he learns when he grows up himself, much less joyful.

That element of joy may ultimately be the most seductive aspect of scheming sociopaths. Though they're primarily driven by boredom, selfishness, and petty jealousy, they nonetheless sometimes have access to the "innocent" satisfaction of a child. In those moments, the inability of children to have meaningful goals is a blessing rather than a curse, as their pleasure needs no outside validation. Their childishness means that they can instrumentalize the trappings of adult life without being really bound by them—they never really get anywhere, but they don't care or need to care. Thus they fulfill the fantasy of the TV sociopath in a particularly enjoyable way, but also in a way that is difficult to take seriously. The scheming sociopath is an indulgence or a release valve, but by no means a model. This stands in contrast with the next category of sociopaths, the climbers. The fantasy the climbers represent is one that is intended to be taken very seriously indeed.

Chapter 2

The Climbers

Many of the adult games that Augustine was so skeptical of remain with us today: the quest for wealth or fame, or public debates and trials won by rhetoric and technicalities rather than truth and justice. Since his time, however, at least one new adult game has emerged—the reality TV show. The genre has its roots in the 1973 PBS miniseries *An American Family*, which followed the everyday life of an average family and was later lampooned in Albert Brooks' 1979 film *Real Life*. Many later incarnations of the genre, such as the Fox series *Cops* and MTV's *The Real World*, maintained the documentary feel of *An American Family*. The real breakthrough for reality TV, however, came from a crucial addition to the reality TV formula: competition. In the 2000s, shows like *Big Brother* and *Survivor* pushed beyond *The Real World*'s preoccupation with how strangers might get along in unfamiliar environments by allowing the group members to vote on who to get rid of every week.

This element of competition, centered on avoiding exclusion rather than positively "winning," seems to have been uniquely effective in encouraging betrayal and petty backbiting, creating a morbid fascination that makes the shows truly addictive. The centrality of exclusion to the model can be seen in the fact that even apparently skill-based shows, such as *America's Next Top Model* or *Hell's Kitchen*, with outside judges determining the winner rather than a vote of one's peers, typically rely on the slow work of "voting people off the island" rather than any kind of positive score-keeping. Some direct physical challenges occur, most notably the contrived physical contests on *Survivor*, but winning one of those has only the indirect effect of temporarily immunizing a contestant from being voted off. A major exception here is *American Idol*, where the audience is able to vote on who to keep rather than who to include—and yet isn't much of the joy of the show found in watching the train wreck auditions early in the season or, until recently, hearing Simon Cowell eviscerate performers again and again?

Following the old dictum that "the truth hurts," the "reality" this genre shows us is primarily a negative one—as indicated in *The Real World's* claim to show "what happens when people stop being nice and start being real." This tagline bears some analysis: what is meant by "nice" here, and what is its negative correlate, the "real"? Niceness presumably indicates some kind of social grace, some attempt to get along with people and get them to like you, and thus "real" behavior is necessarily anti-social, inconsiderate, irresponsible, and gossipy. Indeed, one of *The Real World's* most enduring innovations is the confessional room where participants can vent about the failings of their roommates in total privacy—except for the fact that a national TV audience can hear them. This fundamentally anti-social element is even stronger in competitive shows, which have inspired annual compilations of sociopathic contestants declaring, in what has now become a well-worn cliché, "I'm not here to make friends."

What's wrong with making friends, though? Or more broadly: why might "niceness" be incompatible with the "reality" these shows are portraying? Illustrations from some of the early seasons of *Survivor*—which I watched with a group of friends in my sleepy college town the first couple summers after graduation—might help to make sense of this exclusion of friendship and niceness.

The first example is Rupert Boneham, who quickly emerged as a leader among his fellow jungle inhabitants and supplied much of the camp's food. Ironically, however, his very competence made him appear to be a threat, and he was voted off the island relatively early in the season—although he was ultimately vindicated years later, when he won a prize for being fans' all-time favorite contestant. My friends and I were upset when he was voted off, yet viewed it as retrospectively inevitable: Rupert made himself a target.

Another season saw the emergence of an evil genius named Rob Cesternino who had no apparent skills other than drawing people into "alliances" (i.e., pledges to vote a particular person off the island) on false pretenses. Even though this happened repeatedly and everyone knew what was going on, he managed to finish in the top three. The ultimate runner-up, a capable but naïve contestant who had served essentially as Rob's loyal sidekick throughout the season, even saluted Rob in the end, saying he had learned a lot from him—for instance, he was now planning on watching more TV rather than spending so much time studying foreign languages. And at least among my group of *Survivor* fans, the winner that season, Jenna Morasca, was widely viewed as a lucky usurper, even though she had unexpectedly won many physical challenges, including one guaranteeing her a place in the final two.

Rupert took the contrived premise of "surviving" in a remote location too literally and acted accordingly, doing his best to help the group survive, while Rob saw through the deceptive surface to the actual reality of the situation—a contest to see who can dodge the bullet the longest, which means a contest to see who can do the best job of convincing a critical mass of people to target someone else. Rob was brilliant in that, as even his enemies on the show frequently admitted. He knew "how the game was played" and surely would have won had he made it to the final two. In that context, the actual winner's success in the physical challenges felt like "cheating."

In what kind of "reality" does a lazy bullshitter obviously deserve to win? And in what "reality" has a hard-working caretaker and provider just as obviously made a fatal misstep, while someone who has pulled off a series of physical feats seems like an interloper? I imagine the cynical sides of most of my readers are in agreement with my own in suggesting that the answer here is *"actual* reality." There is a problem with this stance, however, and it's not that it's overly cynical—we are far from living in a meritocracy, and lazy bullshitters triumph over hard workers every day. The problem is the shift from observation to endorsement, from noting that people like Rob do tend to triumph over the Ruperts of this world to claiming that Rob therefore *deserves* to win.

It is this shift that makes my next class of fantasy sociopaths, the climbers, so seductive in their relentless attempt to get ahead—no matter who they wind up hurting. To illustrate this, I'd like to turn away from the low-brow world of reality television to a genre that arose in parallel with reality shows, the high-quality cable drama, and in particular to two shows in that genre that are frequently praised for their painstaking "realism": *Mad Men* and *The Wire*.

From reality television to "realism"

In the 2000s, two contradictory trends changed the shape of American television. On the one hand, the major broadcast networks discovered that reality shows were much cheaper to produce than scripted shows. The result was unsurprising: reality shows came to dominate the airwaves, to such an extent that some observers predicted the end of scripted television, along with literacy, human sympathy, and perhaps civilization as a whole. On the other hand, however, the premium cable network HBO began aggressively developing high-quality, commercial-free drama, finding its first major success in the genre with *The Sopranos*. Other cable channels soon followed suit, leading to a decade that may well have represented the golden age of American television.

The pattern here is familiar. While the offerings available to the common folk over the public airways declined in quality precipitously due to a nihilistic mania for cost-cutting, conditions within the "gated communities" of premium cable networks (which require a separate subscription fee over and above the regular cable bill) were better than ever. As a result of this shift, television suddenly attained a cultural cachet that it never had before. Whereas previously in some "cultured" circles it was a standard (though annoying) boast to claim that one didn't even own a television, now everyone with even minimal cultural pretensions felt guilty for not keeping up with the latest cable drama. And with few exceptions, all these cutting-edge dramas centered on sociopathic characters, including even a charming serial killer.

Why this continual focus on sociopathy? Encouraging identification with evil characters is, of course, a standard move in upstart art forms eager to reach "high-brow" status in bourgeois society. The transition from comic books to "graphic novels" (such as Frank Miller's *The Dark Knight Returns* or Alan Moore's *Watchmen*), for example, was the introduction of the "gritty realism" of the anti-hero in place of the clear divide between good and evil. In that perspective it makes sense that the most successful attempt to establish television as a high-brow art form was HBO's mafia drama *The Sopranos*.

In part, a turn toward "psychologically complex" evil characters serves as a test of liberal empathy—a character like Tony Soprano, who is a ruthless murderer and yet faces typical family problems and insecurities, asks us to set aside simplistic moral judgments and recognize that even the most evil person is still a human being. Someone able to enjoy a show like that surely has a more sophisticated and nuanced grasp on morality than the average professional wrestling fan, for instance, or at least that's what many viewers of such shows tell themselves.

Yet there is another important trait that these characters tend to share that may explain their appeal to their "cultured," upwardly mobile audience at a more visceral and self-interested level: most of these characters are upwardly mobile as well. Tony Soprano, for instance, spends the early seasons of *The Sopranos* gaining and consolidating his position as a mob boss, then spends the later seasons trying to hold onto it. That very straight-forward narrative of moving up the corporate ladder is embedded in a broader narrative where Tony is trying to pull his family up from the working class to the upper class, for instance by buying a "McMansion" in a posh subdivision or sending his daughter to an Ivy League university.

This combination of evil behavior and upward social mobility also occurs in what remains perhaps the most iconic of all the high-quality cable dramas, *Mad Men*. On the one hand, Don Draper represents a fulfillment of the American dream—a farm boy who rose up, through hard work and grit, to become a successful advertising executive—during a particularly optimistic (and retrospectively idealized) period of American history, the early 1960s. Yet on the other hand, the roots of his success are found in an act of identity theft that is almost incomprehensibly sociopathic: when a superior officer in the Korean War is blown to bits by an enemy bomb, he steals his dog tags and thereby gains access to all the privileges the other man's life and service would have entitled him to. What kind of man's first thought, in the split second after witnessing a horrific death, is not to panic, not to head for cover, but to consider how he can take advantage of this situation to raise his social standing?

As I have noted, *Mad Men* is often praised for its realism. Article after article has detailed the obsessive attention to detail of the show's creator, Matthew Weiner, who demands that every stapler and paper clip used on the show be authentic to the milieu of 1960s advertising firms and pores over ancient commuter train schedules to make sure that Don Draper's daily schedule plausibly reflects the lifestyle of a New York executive. Fans have attempted to imitate Weiner in this regard, trying to recapture 1960s fashions and to become conversant with the nuances of mixing cocktails—indeed, I myself recently attended a *Mad Men*-themed cocktail party and applied copious amounts of pomade to my hair in imitation of the show's star. Yet while the rich and distinctive "look" of the show is certainly part of its appeal, I can't help but ask how any of the show's viewers (other than the vanishingly small number of people who really worked in advertising in the era portrayed) would be able to tell the difference if Weiner was faking it. At the end of the day, we must simply take his word for it—and yet every time I've heard a fan mention the show's authenticity, they say it with the conviction of someone who knows firsthand that the show is "real."

One can see a similar dynamic in a show that occupies a very different niche within the ecosystem of high-quality cable dramas, namely *The Wire*. Focusing on the drug culture of Baltimore, *The Wire* portrays an experience that very few of the show's upwardly-mobile viewers have had any contact with at all. In fact, when one scene features a drug dealer explaining the game of chess by reference to the drug trade, one could be forgiven for assuming the real purpose was to familiarize the audience with the drug trade through the more familiar reference point of chess. Yet once again, all the fans I've talked to praise the show's unrelenting realism with all the assurance of someone who grew up on the mean streets. Despite the obvious fantasy elements—such as the flamboyantly gay badass Omar, a cowboy-like figure who robs drug dealers for a living—well-meaning viewers have tended to identify the show as a virtual documentary.

This could be yet another manifestation of white liberals' fantasy of finding some easy and cost-free way to identify with and sympathize with the plight of African-Americans—a fantasy that probably explains, for example, the elevation of the sadistically manipulative film *Precious* to the level of a major Oscar contender and certainly accounts for *The Wire*'s status as the cable drama that everyone feels they *should* watch but also expects to be a distasteful chore (at least before they actually start watching). Given that basically the same fan base reacts in such a similar manner to *Mad Men*'s much "easier" point of identification, however, I believe that something else is at stake in the designation of these shows as amazingly "realistic" by people who have no way of knowing whether they actually are or not.

Just as with reality shows—which probably are "realistic" in the minimal sense of portraying how people would "really" act when placed in their various contrived situations—the "reality" that is at stake here is more fundamental than the surface-level authenticity of office equipment and urban slang. The reality at stake is found in the harsh worldview of both shows, their cynical and unsentimental portrayal of life as a continual power struggle. Like a jaded reality show contestant, nearly every character in *Mad Men* or *The Wire* is "not here to make friends."

Yet while the two genres are at one in their portrayal of life as a game of sociopathic self-advancement, there is one crucial difference between them. Whereas reality show contestants must play according to the pre-given rules in order to win, the characters in high-quality cable dramas can and sometimes must change the rules in their attempt to get ahead. One such character is *Mad Men*'s Peggy Olson, Don Draper's secretary-turned-protégé, who serves as a kind of embodiment of the emerging feminist movement of the early 1960s. The differences between her path and that taken by Don are, in my view, both more and less significant than they might first appear, making a comparison between the two a particularly fruitful starting point for investigating the obstacles facing the upwardly mobile sociopath.

The paradoxes of sociopathic social climbing
While *Mad Men* portrays the social upheavals of the 1960s "from the inside," it does so partly by showing the cluelessness of many of the characters about the huge changes taking place all

around them. The show's star, Don Draper, often stands out for the degree to which he is out of step with the mood of the country, and nowhere is this clearer than in the wake of the assassination of John F. Kennedy. While everyone around him is glued to their TV set, devastated by the tragedy, Don calmly explains to his children the real-world consequences of what has happened: "We have a new President and we're all gonna be sad for a little bit."

This remark certainly reflects Don's profound emotional coldness, but it is also illustrative of the considerable value he places on the impersonal or "objective" element in social structures. For Don, the system "works," or at least should "work," independently of the people moving within it. For instance, the government won't fall apart simply because one particular man was killed—someone else will become president and things will go as normal. That position seems sensible as far as it goes, but his faith in the impersonal extends to a much more fine-grained level. For instance, his entire approach to advertising assumes that there are certain emotional triggers that simply "work" on everyone. He himself demonstrates this point in one of the most well-known scenes in the series, his famous pitch for the Kodak Carousel slide projector, where he delivers a moving speech on the power of nostalgia. Not only do the clients enthusiastically buy his pitch, but he also buys it himself, rushing home to try to intercept his family before they leave for a Thanksgiving trip he had previously begged off. Poignantly (and predictably), by the time he gets there, it is too late.

This attitude can be seen in his choice of wife as well: even though his extramarital affairs reveal a marked preference for strong-willed, intelligent, ambitious brunettes, Don's childish wife Betty is a gorgeous blonde and former model, the gold standard of "objective" (that is, socially-accepted) female attractiveness. Similarly, even though he obviously prefers city life, he opts for the big suburban house that is *de rigueur* for the upwardly mobile white collar worker. If impersonal social expectations are important to him, then so are impersonal social interactions, above all those based in the exchange of money. He repeatedly attempts to buy off people in situations where recourse to money is completely inappropriate, as when he tries to pay his long-lost brother—who has no other family remaining and just wants to reconnect—to get lost, leading to his brother's suicide.

The ultimate triumph of the impersonal, though, comes from Don's stolen identity itself, an identity that can, in his mind, function just as well even if its original bearer is dead and a farm boy previously known as Dick Whitman has taken it up in his stead. This mercenary approach to human identity is a necessary correlate to his ability to buy his own pitch, showing the thorough inner consistency of his worldview: everyone can be manipulated by the same emotional triggers, *including me*, and everyone is interchangeable, *even me*. This nihilism reaches its apex in what may count as Don's only foray into philosophical reflection. Responding to a beatnik who accuses him of manufacturing the "big lie" through his work in advertising, "Well, I hate to break it to you, but there is no big lie. There is no system. The universe is indifferent." The beatnik is despondent in the face of this claim—apparently, for him, the existence of some kind of controlling force, even an evil one, was a necessary comfort.

If Don Draper's "philosophy" is internally consistent, however, his desires are not. Don desperately craves recognition from the very same social system that supposedly does not exist. To return to the discussion of Freud from the previous chapter, this seems to stem from his strange relationship to his father, who conceived him with a prostitute. (His original name, Dick, refers to the body part his mother threatened to cut off if his father got her pregnant.) When his mother dies in childbirth, the midwife takes the baby to his father, who never lets him forget that he's a "whoreson."

In the same episode where he proclaims that the universe is indifferent, we see a series of flashbacks to the visit of a hobo to the Whitman family farm when Dick/Don was a young boy. In conversation with the hobo, he announces that he is a whoreson and assumes that the hobo somehow already knew it—indicating that Dick/Don has reached the desired "mature" state of identifying with his father, though obviously not in a healthy or affirming way, and foreshadowing his later idea that he is simply what people say he is. The hobo contributes to his development, however, both by introducing him to the appeal of simply running away from his responsibilities and living by his wits—strategies Don will use throughout his life—and also by providing him with a new, more impersonal scale of evaluation, namely the sign the hobo leaves on a fencepost indicating that his father is a dishonest man.

Don will continue to seek out more "honest" father figures, fathers who will properly evaluate him according to the "objective" standards of success in which he has proven his worth. His first father figure in the series is his colleague Roger Sterling, who is the first to recognize his creative potential but ultimately disappoints him by divorcing his wife and marrying his secretary—and even worse, Roger falsely credits Don with "advising" him to take this course after misunderstanding something Don said when they were both drunk. His attempted replacement is the eccentric millionaire Conrad Hilton, who meets Don by chance and then begins to "take an interest in him," promising him ever greater successes. Yet one perceived failure on Don's part—based on a "mistake" that is every bit as arbitrary and unaccountable as Hilton's decision to single Don out in the first place—leads to rejection.

Shortly after the disappointment with Hilton, Don makes the bold move of founding a new ad agency out of the ruins of his old one, in a truly exhilarating season finale that showed forth Don's sociopathic genius in all its glory. Surely at this point, I thought as the season drew to a close, Don had finally grown up and taken responsibility for his own identity and self-worth. Yet the next season finds Don a shell of his former self, reduced to a pathetic alcoholic by his wife Betty's decision to trade him in for another man. The fourth season does witness a reflective turn on his part, as the death of the real Don Draper's wife, who had become his closest confidante and his only source of real unconditional love, leads him to resolve to become a better man, more in control of his drinking and his emotions. He keeps a journal, he exercises more, he abstains from casual sex—but when the next crisis comes, he's back to the old impulsive ways that have always served him so well.

This relapse should not be surprising, given that Don's approach to life militates against the development of any real internal life. The rare moments when Don lets down the cold façade reveal that there is very little beneath the surface other than panic, self-pity, or—in his better moments—the kind of cloying sentimentality that allows him to praise the abusive and cruel mother Betty as "so full of love." One can hardly blame him for tearing out the pages of his personal journal and using the notebook to plot the next bold gambit to boost his public image—the flashy play of surfaces is much more exciting than his halting attempts to carve out some space of authenticity.

What this reveals is that Don doesn't really believe his own "philosophy." He does believe in the system, and he believes that it can and will give him the recognition he craves. Surely, he must think, the system that has so lavishly rewarded his creativity and determination is fundamentally good. Such is the paradox of the sociopathic pursuit of social status—even while it requires antisocial behavior on an interpersonal level, its goals remain social, and one must endorse the social system on some level in order for the pursuit of its goals to seem worthwhile. That is the great danger of meritocracy: the people who reach the top of the system are precisely the people who have most completely identified with the system and its demands, creating a vicious circle preventing any actual change. It is no accident that conservatives tend to employ the rhetoric of social mobility so readily, as social climbers generally do not ask questions about the ladder.

This dynamic changes, however, when the social climber is someone who for whatever reason cannot identify with the system as it stands. In *Mad Men's* world, the clearest example of that ambivalent stance toward the system is Peggy Olson, a secretary who becomes a copywriter. Interestingly, her father is almost completely absent from the show—the only mention of him that I have been able to uncover in the series so far is a reference to the fact that he was Norwegian, so that literally his only explicit influence on Peggy comes in the form of her last name.

This lack of any father corresponds to a marked literalism or overidentification with "objective" and impersonal social standards, as illustrated by a sequence of events that initiate her into full-fledged sociopathy. On her first day of work, the seductive office manager, Joan, is amused by how seriously Peggy takes her position as a secretary, informing her that the real goal of the job is to have some fun in the city and then find a husband. Accordingly, Joan sets her up with an appointment to get birth control, where the doctor unfortunately focuses on moral lectures rather than informing her how the drug actually works. Thus she has sex with her co-worker Pete Campbell the first night she is on birth control, before it has time to take effect, and winds up pregnant—yet her belief that she was on birth control and thus *cannot* be pregnant leads her into profound denial that is only punctured when her water breaks.

By this time, Don has made her a full-time copywriter and generally taken on the role of mentor. The only person outside her family to visit her in the hospital after she has given up the child for adoption (and is presumably under observation for major psychological problems), Don offers Peggy a piece of advice that reflects the formative influence of the hobo on his life: "Get out of here and move forward. This never happened. It will shock you how much it never happened." Not as emotionally cold as Don, she is unable to take his advice fully, naturally feeling guilt over abandoning the baby—but also ultimately revealing her decision to give up the baby as a part of her personal power struggle with Pete, who is continually stymied in his effort to get involved in the creative side of the business and is therefore profoundly jealous of his sometime lover.

The way she couches this devastating revelation is itself revealing, however. More than simply stating that she gave away his child—incidentally at a time when Pete and his wife are having difficulty conceiving—she says that she could have shamed him into marrying her, but chose not to. This highlights a dilemma that neither Don nor Pete seriously have to face in their quest for status: "success" for a married woman consists precisely in *not* working in this social milieu. For a man—even a lower-class man like Don, who admittedly would not likely have been able to overcome his class disadvantage without stealing Don Draper's identity—business success and family success (or at least the well-maintained public appearance of family success) go hand-in-hand. Peggy, however, must choose between the two paths.

Though Peggy is arguably a more fully-developed human being than Don, her decision to choose her own personal ambition over social expectations renders her more overtly "anti-social" in the eyes of the world. Her continual anxiety that people will assume she only has her position because of an affair with Don reflects the fact that for many, her position is inherently illegitimate and therefore *must* have been obtained through illegitimate means. At the same time, it reveals the system itself to be anti-social in the way that it effectively prevents ambitious women from forming the deep social bond between mother and child—in Peggy's case encouraging her to deny that she was pregnant (did literally no one in the office think to take her aside and ask if she might be pregnant?) and then actively reject the unwanted child.

This inhospitality to the reality of women's bodily experience is only one of many ways in which the "ladder" is revealed to be one built for men. The very assumption that secretaries will sleep with the male office workers shows that, as seen in the discussion of female characters in the previous chapter, the only roles that are ready-made for women in this system are sex object and servant. Peggy's failure to adhere to the former role, above all when she gains weight as a result of her pregnancy, opens her up to continual abuse (including from her fellow women), and even after she joins the creative team, she is still expected to serve her male co-workers in petty ways.

The continual sexual joking of this "boy's club" presents Peggy with a special dilemma when a freelancer working under her insults her former mentor Joan. Peggy ultimately decides to fire him, but Joan disapproves of that solution, saying that it will only solidify the impression that women are "humorless bitches." Joan reveals that she would have preferred a more feminine, passive-aggressive solution, and some reviewers sided with Joan and concluded that Peggy had made a mistake. The lesson I take away, however, is that as a woman in a position of power she simply can't win—there is no unambiguously "womanly" way to do that job.

Peggy's experience of this contradiction is freeing in many ways, allowing her to participate in the social experimentation of the 1960s more than almost any other character on the show. It also presents a model for social climbing that is necessarily different from that exemplified by Don. His approach, centered on interchangeability, reflects the reality that within a closed, competitive system, it really is a zero-sum game. Don can only get ahead by displacing someone else (above all the original Don Draper), and he can only gain power by taking it away from someone else. There is no "slot" for Peggy in that power struggle, however, and so her advancement within it can only result from the creation of some new space for her. Perhaps as a result of the basic generosity at the root of her success, Peggy tends to be more generous in turn. For instance, she sticks up for the sloppy drunk Freddy, the copywriter who first recognized her creative potential, even after he wets his pants before an important presentation.

At the same time, she does wind up taking Freddy's office after he is sent to rehab, simply because she's the only one bold enough to ask for it. In other words, she does find her place in the power structure, and time will tell how she deals with a temptation that professional women often face—that of wanting to be *the* successful woman in that organization and therefore distrusting other aspiring women as potential rivals. The end of the most recent season seems to be setting up a situation along those lines, as Don marries a secretary with creative ambitions and co-workers begin to speculate that he'll make her a copywriter. The look of concern on Peggy's face could just reflect the worry that a secretary *actually* sleeping her way into a copywriting position would reinforce the perception that Peggy had taken that path. Yet it could just as easily reflect a worry that she's going to be replaced.

The experience of being brought into the system may start with some form of generosity, then, but it does not necessarily inculcate greater generosity of spirit. The person "graciously" let into the inner circle will likely feel like she has more to lose—and her inescapable skepticism about a system that won't allow for direct identification may, in practice, lead to little more than a greater vigilance in avoiding being screwed over. That is to say, the outsider-turned-insider's inability to fully identify with the system may actually provide an even greater incentive to act in the sociopathic ways the system demands. A broken system doesn't just reward broken people—it produces them.

The perils of changing "the game"

While Peggy faced significant challenges in moving up through the system, she did have one advantage: she was in some sense "part" of the system, even if her role was subordinate. She would never have had a chance to become a copywriter if she hadn't been in regular contact with the creative team as Don's secretary, for instance. More broadly, though the game of competition among the young women for the best husband has a certain autonomy, it is nonetheless incorporated into the broader game of male social advancement.

More challenges arise for someone so far removed from the center of power that genuine social advancement seemingly requires the leap from one social system to another one entirely. That is the situation that faces *The Wire*'s Stringer Bell, who desperately wants to make the transition from an inner-city drug kingpin to a legitimate businessman—specifically, a property developer. In many ways, his strategy is similar to that of Don Draper, relying heavily on impersonality and specifically the impersonality of money. Yet his situation is more complicated. Not only does he face the obstacle of the segregation between inner-city African-Americans and the affluent whites he must deal with to fulfill his goals. More than that, even his money, since it was earned through criminal enterprise, must be actively *made* "impersonal" by means of the money laundering carried out by his slimy lawyer. That lawyer in turn represents his only real point of contact with the legitimate social circles he hopes to enter, as all his other "social networking" opportunities are among criminals.

One of the most amusing aspects of Stringer's character is the way that he anticipates his legitimate status in his lifestyle. When the show opens, Stringer is the second-in-command in the criminal organization of his best friend Avon Barksdale—yet again, the sociopathic social climber lacks a father figure or indeed any apparent biological family at all—and handles the business end of things. He successfully keeps his hands clean by mostly avoiding any direct (or at least indictable) connection with violence, and he even takes economics courses at the community college, treating the drug dealing operation like any other business enterprise. Even his dress signals his aspirations, as he favors "business casual" clothes over typical street gang attire, occasionally including the infamous "Cosby sweaters" worn by the very embodiment of African-American upward mobility, Dr. Cliff Huxtable of *The Cosby Show*.

A large part of what allows Stringer to indulge in these fantasies of being a legitimate businessman is the fact that Avon and his various enforcers mostly handle the violence necessary to maintain their drug empire. This all changes, however, when Avon and most of the rest of the organization are put in prison, leaving only Stringer to keep the enterprise alive. At this point, he demonstrates his willingness to make the kind of "tough choices" that sociopathic leaders are so often praised for, such as ordering the murder of everyone, including young teenagers, who might inform on the members of the organization who remain out of jail. Yet lacking muscle, the Barksdale operation steadily loses ground in the public housing towers it previously dominated and is faced with a seemingly fatal blow when the towers are demolished.

Seemingly Stringer must either gain new territory or go out of business, and yet he lacks the muscle necessary to pull it off. How he responds to this situation of weakness is through an ingenious solution: rather than engaging in futile violence to try to improve his position in the drug trade, he attempts to make Baltimore's drug trade less violent. He begins, ironically, by taking some advice from Jimmy McNulty, the homicide detective who was behind the investigation into the Barksdale operation and who becomes obsessed with taking down Stringer after he escapes prosecution. McNulty tells one of the middle managers of the operation that the police don't really care about the drugs as such—it's the murders (or, as Baltimore police slang charmingly puts it, "the bodies") that force law enforcement to get involved.

In his weakened position, Stringer takes this message to heart, ordering his dealers, despite their strong resistance to the idea, never to engage in violence to defend "corners." Over time, he convinces the other operators in Baltimore to come together in a drug "co-op" that will allow them to pool their resources and purchase bigger shipments of higher-quality drugs in exchange for agreeing to end turf battles. In true corporate style, the co-op members have periodic meetings in a hotel conference room, where meetings are conducted according to *Robert's Rules of Order*. Overall, Stringer convinces his fellow drug-dealers to turn "the game," as they all call the drug business, into a positive-sum rather than zero-sum game—by collaborating and keeping violence to a minimum, everyone can make more money and avoid drawing the attention of law enforcement.

These changes, making the drug culture of Baltimore more "economically rational," correspond to Stringer's greatest successes in shifting to legitimate lines of business. With the help of his lawyer, he buys up properties to turn into condos. Yet he continually runs into trouble in his new role as a property developer, applying a street gang mentality to legitimate business—for instance, threatening contractors over routine delays and cost overruns—at the same time that he is trying to apply business principles to "the game." Stringer also shows himself to be shockingly naïve, allowing a corrupt congressman to convince him that he can get his way by literally walking into the federal building and handing a bribe to an official (who turns out to be the congressman's own plant). No classroom had prepared him for the realities of playing the game of "legitimate" business.

At the same time, circumstances conspire to undermine Stringer's more rational approach to drug dealing. Avon gets out of prison, for instance, and deeply disapproves of the non-violent co-op system, believing that it makes his organization look soft and weak. More seriously, a new drug lord named Marlo begins his rise—a character so sadistic and just plain *evil* that one almost suspects that he was created solely to disprove the well-meaning liberal fans who praised *The Wire* for its supposed complete moral ambiguity. The result of these tensions between the approaches of Stringer and Avon is that the Barksdale organization self-destructs through their mutual betrayal. True to form, Avon betrays Stringer to two characters who have an old-fashioned grudge against him and refuse to be bought off, while Stringer betrays Avon to the police before he can begin his offensive against Marlo.

After Stringer's fall, the evil Marlo eventually games the co-op system to gain direct access to their supplier and thereby become the sole drug lord of Baltimore. His rise to power is deeply ironic when compared to Stringer's attempt. Marlo also evades police attention for a long time, for instance, but not through reducing the violence—instead, he has two dedicated enforcers who murder with impunity and then "disappear" the bodies in the boarded up buildings that Stringer might have turned into condos. The police catch him right as he gains his hold on power, but as he sits in jail, the preternaturally calm Marlo explodes in anger when he finds out someone has been trash-talking him and his underlings didn't report it to him. Finally, he winds up going free due to the compromised nature of the investigation spearheaded by McNulty (a point I will return to in the next chapter) and is actually *forced* into the role of a property developer.

In short, Marlo destroys everything that Stringer created and nevertheless gets everything Stringer ever dreamed of. For Marlo, however, the legitimate system is the worst kind of prison, and the last scene in which he appears shows him unceremoniously ditching a business meeting in order to beat up a random street dealer—and in case we hadn't already gotten the message, he literally tastes the blood on his fingers before the camera cuts away.

What lessons can we derive from Stringer's fate? Unlike Peggy's situation of being unable to identify fully with the system she has entered, Stringer's problem seems to be that he overidentifies with the system he is trying to enter—and at the same time, he fails to take seriously the system he is still actually a part of. He is too trusting in the legitimate businessmen and politicians he deals with as he tries to become a major property developer (a role that the detectives investigating him joke is even worse than being a drug dealer), and the root of that is that he is too trusting in his own mastery of business logic.

In his dealings within the drug culture itself, he believes that economic rationality can win out, so that every problem can be solved through persuasion and mutually beneficial agreements. If someone fails to conform to that logic by acting according to the laws of personal loyalty and personal vendettas that actually structure the culture of street gangs, Stringer assumes that person must be an idiot who can be easily tricked and manipulated—or, failing that, who must be stopped by *someone else* (as in his decision to hand Avon over to the police).

Though Stringer's situation is structurally similar to Peggy's, he makes the mistake of believing that he somehow already belongs to the culture of legitimate business. Peggy could never make the mistake of believing she had actually become a man, but Stringer is blinded by the seemingly objective qualification of having money. Just as Peggy is absolutely certain that she *can't* be pregnant because she's on birth control, so also is Stringer absolutely certain that he *can't* be just another African-American kid from the street because he has money and a nice sweater. Peggy received her wake-up call that she was still limited by her female body in the form of an unexpected baby, while Stringer only gets his wake-up call in the seconds before his death, when he gives up trying to broker a deal and yells at his murderers to get it over with. In this moment, he has faced the fact that he is still effectively part of the street gang system, a system that is irreducibly violent. And as subsequent events show, Stringer's attempt to change the system from within only opened up the space for a much more violent force to emerge, namely Marlo.

To summarize, then, both Peggy and Stringer have an initially favorable view of the system they are entering. That naïveté is quickly shattered in Peggy's case, while it leads to Stringer's downfall. As for the seeming "insiders," Don and Marlo, both believe in their respective systems so completely that their very success opens them up to shattering disappointments whenever anything goes wrong. Don becomes a panicked emotional wreck on the rare occasions when things don't go his way, while Marlo indulges in impotent anger when it becomes clear that even being the undisputed king of the Baltimore drug trade can't keep people from trash-talking you on the street. Marlo's exclamation in response to this humiliation is a sentiment that Don could endorse: "My *name* is my *name*."

While this section began with the impression that there is a huge gap between the social systems Stringer tries to navigate, Marlo's fate shows that they are more tightly integrated than it might seem. After all, Marlo's name would have been permanently vindicated had he been convicted of the dozens of murders the police uncovered in the boarded-up houses, yet McNulty's extra-legal investigation made the evidence against Marlo inadmissible in a trial. In order to save face and avoid the exposure of McNulty's actions, the justice system offers Marlo a free pass as long as he leaves the drug trade—preserving the system's good name while dooming Marlo to the intolerable fate of looking to all the world like just another punk. Marlo's response is to engage in completely random violence, as though he wants to get caught, or in other words, as though he wants his toughness to become official again after the police deprived him of any way of clearing his "name."

Even Marlo, the most sociopathic climber of them all, wants the approval of the system—he's accepted the path for advancement left open to him, a life of crime, and excelled to the greatest possible degree. In that perspective, the fact that he has to live with his tarnished name simply to allow the system to save face is a profound injustice. Yet as my next class of sociopaths— the enforcers—demonstrate, when the credibility of the system itself is at stake, none of its promises matter any longer. For this "highest" class of sociopaths, the only way to save our broken society is to break it even more.

Chapter 3

The Enforcers

A scene from *The Wire* provides a convenient way of both consolidating my argument up to this point and setting up the problem with which this chapter will be occupied. In this scene, D'Angelo Barksdale, a young cousin of Avon Barksdale and a (recently demoted) management figure in the organization, comes upon two of his younger workers playing chess, apparently with no regard for the rules. When he tries to correct them, they say that they don't know how to play chess and they're just using the chess pieces to play checkers. D'Angelo, declaring that chess is a "better game," sets out to explain the game by analogy to the drug trade.

Some of the metaphors are strained—for instance, the notion that the rook is the "stash" where they keep their drug inventory—but others are very clear. Avon is the king, for instance, meaning he is simultaneously the most important figure in the organization and the one who apparently contributes the least. Stringer, by contrast, is the queen, the powerful piece that does the most work, albeit still at the service of the apparently less capable king. Finally, they themselves identify with the pawns, and they are very interested when D'Angelo tells them that while pawns are usually the first to be killed off, they can, if they endure and plow forward, be promoted. Yet they are disappointed to learn that they can only reach as high as the queen, and when they ask him why, D'Angelo simply says, "The king stays the king."

This scene itself invites an analogy to the classes of fantasy sociopath I have defined so far. The schemers, who deploy adult privileges for childish ends, are like the young drug dealers playing checkers with chess pieces. They get some satisfaction, certainly, but checkers only provides so much entertainment. They could always use the chess pieces in another way, but it's a near-certainty that the pieces' intended use is in fact the "better game"—after all, what are the odds that they'll come up with a game that's more sophisticated than chess? It is admittedly still a game, as the cartoonishly ambitious characters on *30 Rock* imply, but it at least lasts longer and provides more variety than whatever other game the kids might make up.

The shift from the scheming sociopath to the climber is not just the shift from checkers to chess, however. It is the shift from viewing the game with detachment from the outside to identifying with those poor put-upon pawns. This means first of all accepting that one's goal is to get ahead as far as possible, if not strictly for the sake of survival, then at least for the sake of being something other than an insignificant piece in some forgotten corner of the board. Perhaps even more importantly, though, it means accepting that the highest rank one can attain is that of the most powerful and versatile servant of the king.

Stringer Bell, as the "queen" of the Barksdale organization, does often go behind Avon's back, but it's always for the sake of strengthening the operation and almost always a move that he more or less sincerely believes Avon will come to see the wisdom of in time. Being the "queen" is his highest goal in this context: at no point does he unequivocally claim leadership for himself or try to get rid of Avon. Even Stringer's decision to give Avon up to the police to keep him from engaging in a destructive drug war is ultimately in the service of what's "good for business"—Avon will still nominally be king, but his scope of action must be limited to keep him from damaging the organization's prospects. Ironically, at the same time, Avon is planning his own betrayal, giving permission for two highly dangerous characters with a grudge against Stringer to kill him, lest they ruin Avon's reputation and thereby permanently cut off his supply of drugs.

As every chess player knows, even the queen is expendable if it means avoiding checkmate.

One question that *The Wire* leaves unanswered is how one becomes a king. Essentially all the major gang leaders are already established, at least as the head of their own particular group of loyalists, by the time the viewer meets them. Marlo's quest to rule the drug trade in Baltimore might be close, but even then he's not really *becoming* a king, simply expanding his pre-existing power. The only real struggle for leadership is the mayoral election, in which the ultimate winner, Carcetti, immediately starts positioning himself for a run as governor so he can get the hell out of Baltimore—being mayor, which means managing a rolling disaster, apparently does not feel much like being a king. Nor in fact does Marlo's consolidation of power over the drug trade constitute much of a triumph, as he quickly discovers that his power applies only within a subordinate part of the overarching system of Baltimore and his seemingly absolute power really only extends as far as that larger system is willing to tolerate.

Does Baltimore—and the broader society of which it presents a microcosm—have any genuine kings? In one scene, Omar, the cowboy-like robber of drug dealers, taunts some enemies who have tried and failed to kill him with one of the most memorable lines of the series: "Come at the king, you best not miss." This line could be read as a setup for a later scene in which Omar takes a shot at Avon and misses, but I think it's interesting to take Omar seriously as a potential "king," or at least the kind of king that's possible within a system like Baltimore.

What makes Omar so compelling is that he makes his own rules—he is a truly sovereign individual in that sense, acting only according to his own self-imposed ethical "code." Omar is far from sociopathic, as he is capable of a fierce loyalty that is not focused primarily on family members. Much of his plot arc is in fact dominated by his attempt to avenge the torture and death of his lover at the hands of Avon's gang. Yet there is a sense in which the cartoonish Omar is similar to the scheming sociopaths: his activity doesn't lead anywhere. He enjoys "the game" *as* a game more than almost any other player, but there is no way he can win other than by cashing out and retiring. His behavior always remains parasitic on the system he believes himself to be above, and the more successful he is, the more certain his death becomes. This seductive figure ultimately represents a kind of total nihilism, and the show's writers emphasize this dead-end aspect of Omar by giving him an anti-climactic and even pathetic death. The fantasy of Omar is attractive as entertainment, but like that of the scheming sociopaths, it's not a fantasy you'd want to live out in real life.

Using Omar as the template, however, there does seem to be at least one other sovereign individual, one other self-appointed king: Jimmy McNulty, the "natural police" whose passion for the job sets much of the action of the series in motion. Like Omar, McNulty disregards the social rules that bind others, but he doesn't do so in service of a self-appointed moral code. Instead, he breaks the rules precisely in service of *the job*. His ultimate goal is to turn the Baltimore Police Department into what it claims to be: an organization devoted to the real work of solving and preventing crimes, rather than a bureaucracy devoted to processing crime statistics in misleading ways in order to support various political ambitions.

This fantasy of suspending the normal rules in order to *do what needs to be done* is an attractive one—and, in contemporary society, an increasingly prevalent one. As more and more organizations, in government and business alike, seem to be self-perpetuating bureaucracies with little connection to their original goals, the fantasy of a brave leader coming in, shaking things up, and setting things right is compelling. It's even more convincing when that brave leader shows he's for real by being self-sacrificing: working long hours, taking low pay, even neglecting his family out of his passionate devotion to the cause. This leader, so the fantasy goes, is so devoted to the goals of the organization that he's willing to break all the organization's own rules in service of it, so driven by moral conviction that he neglects his most fundamental moral obligations. Such behavior will win you a place at the right hand of the Lord—or, failing that, a flattering profile in the *New York Times* Sunday magazine.

It is this fantasy of breaking society's rules for the sake of saving society itself that I will be investigating in this chapter, under the heading of the "enforcers." While school administrators seem to dominate real-life examples of this particular class of sociopaths, boldly firing teachers in order to further the cause of education, the majority of examples on television come from law enforcement. While police procedurals have always been popular, in recent years there has been a tendency toward "rogue" police units as on *The Shield*, made up of Dirty Harry-like officers who take the law into their own hands. As the reference to the Dirty Harry films shows, this theme has never been entirely absent, but its more recent currency likely stems from the so-called "War on Terror"—as demonstrated by the popularity of the terrorism-based show *24*. Accordingly, I will begin this chapter by investigating a character who is surely one of the most fantastical of all the fantasy sociopaths: Jack Bauer.

The lawless lawman

As difficult as it is to imagine now, *24*, now virtually synonymous with the "War on Terror," was actually created and put into production by the Fox television network before the terrorist attacks of September 11, 2001. According to online sources, the pilot was filmed in March 2001 and filming on the rest of the episodes—Fox originally only ordered 13 of the 24 implied by the show's title—began in July of that year. The initial innovation of the show was not its focus on terrorism, but rather its "real-time" nature, where all events unfold within a 24-hour period synchronized with an on-screen clock. Focused on Counter Terrorism Unit (CTU) agent Jack Bauer, the show's original theme could be defined as the unique challenges he faces in maintaining work-life balance—for instance, how to cope after someone kidnaps his family in an attempt to blackmail him into assassinating a presidential candidate, Senator David Palmer.

While the first season premiered less than three months after the 9/11 attacks, it still feels like an artifact of the "happier" 1990s. The primary villains are not Islamic terrorists, but rather Serbian nationalists seeking revenge for an operation in the now virtually forgotten war in Kosovo, an operation that Senator Palmer helped plan and Jack helped carry out. This political irrelevance may be that first season's saving grace, as the show's writers clearly began to strain under the weight of the political debates over terrorism and especially torture that 24 was made to carry as the Bush administration wore on. The focus throughout remains on the personal cost Jack's devotion to his job exacts, above all in the final plot twist where his wife is revealed to have been killed by a CTU mole.

If the theme of the enforcer's sacrifice of family for his job is thus brought out in an incredibly heavy-handed way, so also is the ineffectiveness of the bureaucracy within which he must work. The Counter Terrorism Unit, a (thankfully!) fictional law enforcement agency, is made up primarily of incompetents, obstructionist bureaucrats, and a truly amazing number of moles—at least one per season. America's front line against terrorism turns out to be incapable of preventing any terrorist attack at all, including on one occasion *against its own office*. This situation is particularly appalling given that the universe of 24 is orders of magnitude more dangerous than our own, with a wide range of terrorist groups operating freely within U.S. borders, killing off presidents, routinely using WMDs (including nuclear bombs), and generally showing themselves to be much more effective than any actual-existing terrorist organization I'm aware of. Even worse: the government itself sometimes foments terrorist attacks to further its own agenda.

In this context, which in its simplistically overdone way is as hopeless as *The Wire*'s Baltimore, Jack emerges as essentially the only person capable of making CTU and the U.S. government as a whole fulfill their base-level duty of protecting the physical safety of the population. He has no patience for more metaphysical concepts of "national security" that allow for the possibility that a terrorist attack might be beneficial in the long run if it spurs the country to fight a necessary war. The way he understands his job is refreshingly straightforward: to prevent terrorist attacks by any means necessary.

Armed with that simple principle, Jack is able to discard all others. As a result, the list of his crimes is truly overwhelming. He regularly violates chain of command, contradicting even direct orders from the president—indeed, sometimes even in the president's presence. He routinely tortures terror suspects, including at one point his own brother. He recruits ordinary citizens to help him with his often rogue operations, invariably resulting in their deaths. He chops off his partner's hand in order to prevent a biological weapon from taking out a school. He shoots a long-time colleague dead to keep him from killing a former terrorist who holds out the promise of a final end to terrorism. He breaks into the Chinese embassy, risking a world war to gain access to a suspect. He kidnaps the president and holds him at gunpoint. He kills his own father when he is revealed to be aiding terrorist plots. He even takes a plane hostage because... it would somehow prevent an attack in a way that I honestly can't remember at this point.

Jack Bauer is, in short, the Eric Cartman of rogue law enforcement. Whatever crime another Dirty Harry type has committed, Jack has done worse. Indeed, few of the show's *terrorists* can match him for sheer violence. Yet all this is done in the service of his country and in fact in service of the very *survival* of his country. Given that he is apparently the only man on earth unambiguously dedicated to that goal, it is very fortunate that his gut instincts are almost invariably correct—and that he is apparently the only accurate marksman alive.

By usurping power at every turn, Jack certainly fills the prototype of the "king" drawn from *The Wire*. Yet his focus on physical survival reveals him to be more than just a self-appointed "king": he is also a father figure, willing to do anything to protect his metaphorical family, i.e., the American people. True to the moral reversal inherent in the figure of the enforcer, his very failure to protect his own biological family, above all in the death of his wife, only throws into sharper relief his absolute dedication to protecting his metaphorical family. Indeed, Jack is willing even to give his own life to protect the family of his country, most dramatically in an episode where he is tortured to the point of clinical death and then revived.

This fatherly aspect of Jack Bauer is the point at which his fantasy is the most powerful: he is the perfect father, the father with no agenda other than being a father. His violent tactics are a pure means to the end of protecting the national family and do not, for instance, reflect a violent or abusive personality. His constant insubordination is a pure means as well, rather than an attempt to gain power or position for himself within the organization—in fact, he regularly "resigns" from CTU mid-mission so as to be able to pursue his rogue operations more freely. This stands in sharp contrast to the criminal parents I discussed in chapter one, the drug-dealers Walter White of *Breaking Bad* and Nancy Botwin of *Weeds*. While they justify their criminal behavior initially as a lamentably necessary way to provide for their family, it becomes clear as their respective stories unfold that they are actually in it for the thrills and the feeling of power it brings. Even after the strict necessity disappears, they continue in their criminal path, whereas presumably Jack Bauer wants nothing more than for his job to become obsolete.

It also stands in contrast to my initial example of the enforcer, *The Wire*'s McNulty. For him, insubordination is a way of proving his superiority, exposing his bosses as empty suits. There is also a real sense in which police work is an addiction for McNulty, and if his attempts to do satisfying and authentic police work are frustrated—as they are most of the time within Baltimore's crumbling police bureaucracy—he turns to other addictions as well, such as alcohol and promiscuous sex. He sacrifices his family to the job in a much different sense than Jack Bauer does, as his alternating (and even overlapping) bouts of obsessive police work and self-destructive behavior compel his wife to divorce him. More than neglecting his family for the sake of his job, he even actively instrumentalizes his children, at one point assigning them to tail Stringer Bell and take down his license plate number while they're out shopping (an activity in which they are already very well-trained).

That incident reflects McNulty's broader obsession with Stringer, which only intensifies after he escapes prosecution in the initial Barksdale bust. For McNulty, Stringer's continued freedom isn't a miscarriage of justice—it's a personal insult. His monomaniacal pursuit of Stringer threatens to alienate his closest colleagues, and when called out on his insubordination, arrogance, and lack of loyalty to people who have helped him, he declares: "Fuck loyalty!" This self-obsession can also work in the other direction, as when a fellow officer, Kima Greggs, is shot in the course of the Barksdale investigation. Given that he started the investigation, McNulty feels responsible for Kima's fate and begins to believe this case isn't worth the price. What is particularly revealing is the consequence he draws from this: since McNulty isn't into it anymore, they should make the arrests they can make and fold up the operation. His commanding officer points out, however, that Kima is every bit as dedicated to the case as he is, a thought that seems not to have occurred to the self-obsessed McNulty.

While the "father-protector" element of the enforcer fantasy is not as prominent in McNulty's case, he does become a kind of fatherly mentor to Kima later in the series. Over the course of several heart-to-heart talks, he instructs her on how to cope with a partner who is unsupportive of her love for police work—and on how to cope with the emotional burden of infidelity.

One can see a similar mentorship in the final seasons of 24, when Jack Bauer initiates FBI agent Renee Walker into the ways of patriotic torture. Unlike in the case of Don Draper's mentorship of Peggy, however, the fact that the protégé is a woman doesn't seem particularly problematic. After all, the entire point of the enforcer character is to sacrifice one's personal attachments and morals for the greater good, which means that the antisocial choice to neglect family duties is actually expected and thus does not introduce a conflict. There are admittedly far fewer female enforcer characters—one thinks of Glenn Close's role as the captain of the rogue unit on *The Shield* or as a law-breaking lawyer in *Damages*, Kyra Sedgwick's character on *The Closer*, or, reaching further back, Helen Mirren's homicide detective character on *Prime Suspect*—yet those who do exist seem generally to present less of an "issue" than an upwardly mobile woman might. Just as women in more recent adult cartoons are equally capable of being petty schemers, so also are women complete equals when it comes to violating the law for the sake of the law.

More central to the enforcer character, however, is the element of being the "king," an element that in McNulty's case comes to a head in the final season, where steep budget cuts make the burdens of dealing with the police bureaucracy truly intolerable. After being forced to take the bus to a crime scene, McNulty snaps and decides to tamper with the body of a dead homeless man to make it appear to be a murder, ultimately manufacturing a fictional serial killer who is supposedly stalking Baltimore's homeless population. Mayor Carcetti, who had previously cut the police budget in order to give the money to the schools, opens up unlimited funding to help catch McNulty's serial killer. McNulty is then put in charge of the investigation and effectively becomes king of the police department, encouraging other officers to use the resources and overtime for their own cases and charge it to his investigation's account.

Predictably, this crazy plan has some negative fall-out. First of all, it inspires a copy-cat killer, so that McNulty has blood on his hands. Second, it compromises the primary investigation that McNulty wants to fund, the one that ultimately brings down Marlo. Though their evidence is bullet-proof, it is also inadmissible, because they could not seek a warrant without revealing McNulty's deception. Finally, it leads to the effective end of McNulty's career. His superiors don't feel they can reveal what McNulty has done without permanently destroying their credibility, and so they opt to cover his tracks while consigning him to an undesirable position and permanently forbid him from doing any investigative work. The copycat killer provides them with a convenient scapegoat when he confesses to all the "murders," allowing the mayor to save face and declare victory, and they also manage to blackmail Marlo into leaving the drug trade (even if only temporarily) without risking a trial that would reveal McNulty's doings.

The end result of McNulty's rogue operation, then, is simply to reinforce the opportunistic bureaucracy's power—in fact, the final montage of the series portrays Carcetti as the governor of Maryland and the police commissioner who oversaw the "serial killer" investigation as the chief of the state police—and deprive the department of one of its most dedicated and talented officers. This is only the culmination of the fundamental irony of McNulty's actions. Most notably, his driving focus for the first three seasons is to catch Stringer Bell, who is arguably the person who is doing the most to make the drug trade less violent, i.e., to concretely reduce crime in Baltimore (rather than reducing crime *statistics*).

That is to say, there is a way in which *The Wire* portrays the kind of good police work McNulty is obsessed with as profoundly unsuited to its setting. This is most pronounced in the story of another of the "kings" portrayed within the police department, Bunny Colvin, a district commander who comes up with a brilliant way to reduce drug-related crime: legalize drugs. Designating an abandoned part of his district a free zone for drug trafficking, he manages to restore some semblance of law and order to the rest of the area. Like McNulty, Colvin is in part motivated by frustration—his crisis moment comes when his superiors explicitly order him to tamper with statistics to create the appearance of a significant decrease in crime—and by pride, as he is nearing retirement and wonders whether his work as a police officer has done any concrete good. As in McNulty's case, the city manages to wrap up his rogue operation in a face-saving way while destroying Colvin's career.

No matter how radically the rogue agent acts to bring the institution back in line with its own goals, it seems, the institution can recover and return to its old path. Indeed, it is stronger than ever, having expelled the dissenter. A similar logic can be seen in 24 as well, as Jack Bauer's heroic actions serve ultimately to empower the hopelessly compromised and mole-ridden Counter-Terrorism Unit and to boost the political fortunes of presidents who, more often than not, turn out to be criminal conspirators themselves.

The paradox here is similar to that faced by the climbers: even by rebelling against a failing social order, the enforcer winds up reinforcing it. Their anti-social behavior—their insubordination, their betrayal of their families, their violence and law-breaking—is all reabsorbed into the social order, just as the sociopathic social climber becomes the most powerful and dedicated servant of the social order. Both the climber and the enforcer have escaped the trap of the schemer, who can have no meaningful goals, but the price they've paid is that their goal is ultimately defined by the broader social order.

The climbers believe they're perfectly self-seeking, yet they let the social order completely define what "self-seeking" means, i.e., what it means to succeed. On the other side, the enforcers believe they're cutting through the meaningless bureaucracy to serve real social needs, but those needs are determined by ideals inculcated by the bureaucracies themselves: could the idea of "police work" exist without an actual-existing police force, or could the idea of "national security" exist without the nation? Both the climbers and the enforcers, in the last analysis, idealize the impersonal social order and hence wind up being in a sense more "pro-social" than any well-meaning average person.

The reason these two types of sociopath can be so paradoxically pro-social is that the broken social order is itself profoundly *anti*-social. Rather than productively mediating our social encounters, it gums them up through cultural awkwardness. Rather than providing us with meaningful shared goals, it gestures toward those goals in support of a self-perpetuating system that constantly undercuts them. Its upper echelons need to be filled in by sociopathic climbers because the system is inherently sociopathic. It needs to be periodically bailed out by sociopathic enforcers because it is itself ultimately lawless. This means that our culture-wide fascination with these sociopaths is not sophisticated or rebellious or countercultural—rather, it serves only to reinforce our collective Stockholm Syndrome.

At this point, all may seem to be lost. The fantasy of the sociopath, it seems, is a pure delusion that serves only to reinforce our acquiescence to a destructive system. That conclusion may well turn out to be correct, but in my view it is too obvious to be fully satisfying. Is there any moment of redemption in these fantasies, anything that genuinely fulfills the promise of freedom from current social constraints?

A hint of a possible way forward here may be an aspect of

McNulty's character that sets him apart from the noble Jack Bauer and in a way hearkens back to the joyfully sociopathic schemers: his selfish motives. He doesn't do police work primarily out of deep moral convictions or a devotion to justice. He does police work because he's "natural police." He does it because it's the only thing that truly satisfies him, and for the most part he's willing to deal with the destructive side-effects of his addiction. The institution of the police is necessary to support his work, but he is not truly working for the sake of the institution nor for the sake of advancing within it (except to reach the level where he can do meaningful investigation).

With this in mind, I'd like to turn now to two characters who push this element of selfish indifference to an extreme—namely, Dexter and House. My goal in doing so is to see if they might offer a way forward to a form of sociopathy that could provide any kind of guide to what, in the eyes of the current system, would be the most profoundly anti-social behavior of all: building an alternative.

Serial murder as community service

The title character of *Dexter*, by contrast with those discussed in the previous section, is not a law enforcement agent. Instead, he supplements police efforts in two ways. First, he works as a blood spatter analyst for the Miami Metro Police homicide department, displaying a true gift for reconstructing the events leading up to a victim's death. Second, he also works as a serial killer, but with a clever twist: he only kills those who are factually guilty of murder but have somehow escaped prosecution. In other words, he both helps the police catch killers and "takes care of" those who elude capture.

Yet Dexter's efforts as a serial killer are not intended primarily as vigilante justice. He really does have a lust for violence, stemming from witnessing his own mother's death and then spending days locked in a room with her dismembered body. His father Harry, a police officer, notices Dexter's destructiveness and anti-social behavior grow throughout his childhood and develops an elaborate plan to keep him from destroying himself. First, he teaches Dexter social skills, using the rough guide of telling him to always say the exact opposite of how he really feels. More importantly, however, believing that Dexter's thirst for blood is never going to go away, Harry instills in Dexter an elaborate "Code" to guide his killing. The first rule is not to get caught, and he uses his experience with forensics to help Dexter learn how not to leave a trace. Second, he must only kill those who are deserving of death, and here again his skills as a police investigator prove invaluable.

Dexter's Code, then, is directed first of all at survival, then at giving him an outlet for his irresistible violent urges—and only then at something like vigilante justice. He is filling in the gaps left by the police bureaucracy, which in the show's world appears to have no major gaping holes (other than letting a serial killer like Dexter onto the payroll), but unlike Jack Bauer or McNulty, he ultimately doesn't care about justice or police work. This is because, at least when the series begins, he doesn't really care about *anything*. Aside from fulfilling his murderous desires, his only gut level emotional connections are to his family: his sister Debra, also a member of the police force, and his father, already long dead at the beginning of the series, who frequently appears to Dexter as a kind of embodiment of the Code. (In fact, the degree to which Dexter's internal "Harry" seems to be autonomous of Dexter's own thought processes strikes me as a manifestation of mental illness almost as troubling as the violent impulses themselves.)

As we've seen, family loyalties are perfectly compatible with sociopathy, particularly when, as in this case, one of the family members is actually one's own mental projection. Dexter himself seems to regard his attachment to his sister as insufficient counterevidence to his overall inability to connect with people or indeed to feel any genuine human emotion. In a running monologue, he continually wonders it is like to *really* feel sadness or whatever other emotion instead of merely performing it as he does. He is generally well-liked by his coworkers and even has a girlfriend (Rita) when the series opens, but these relationships are purely instrumental, part of Harry's plan to make Dexter seem normal so as not to fit the "quiet and keeps to himself" cliché of a serial killer.

All of this makes for an extremely morbid premise, perhaps the peak of the trend toward unsympathetic characters in TV drama. When the broadcast network CBS announced during the 2007-2008 U.S. television writers strike that it would air edited reruns of *Dexter*, which normally runs on the premium cable network Showtime, the conservative advocacy group that protested the decision may have had a point. No matter how much the explicit on-screen violence is edited out, it's impossible to edit out the fundamental fact that *Dexter* is a show that incites its viewers to root for a cold-blooded serial murderer.

Yet it's worth asking what the audience is rooting for him to do. On the one hand, yes, one is admittedly hoping for Dexter not to get caught. In addition, in his battles with other "worse" serial killers (whose choice of victims is determined by some pathology rather than the Code), one would normally prefer for Dexter to win. On the other hand, however, the show is asking the audience to root for Dexter in his usually abortive attempts to become a "real boy," that is, to make some kind of authentic human connection.

These efforts take place in two different ways. The first happens when Dexter tells someone of his identity as a serial killer, thus starting the relationship on his own terms. In the second season, he does this with a secret lover who turns out to be a firebug and nearly kills his girlfriend Rita's children. Having learned his lesson, in the third season he inducts a newfound friend into the ways of the Code—but again, things spiral out of control as Dexter's protégé goes rogue and murders a professional rival who was guilty of no crime greater than pissing him off.

This second example produced one of the least satisfying plotlines, in my opinion, but it is at least interesting in what it reveals about the Code: it is not purely solipsistic, but constitutes a kind of social order unto itself. For the most part, it's a one-man social order encompassing only Dexter, but that is just a contingent fact. His protégé did not wind up taking it seriously, but he could have—as in fact a later protégé does. To return to the Freudian model in which one must identify with the father to be inducted into a broader social order, Dexter has successfully identified with his father, but much too closely. The result is that he is not inducted into an impersonal social world, but rather into Harry's vision of how Dexter must negotiate his way through that world. While in principle someone else could follow these rules, in practice Dexter follows them as *Harry's* Code and even relates to them through a kind of projected ghost of their institutor.

In this context, Dexter's attempts to achieve some kind of connection to someone else by "normal" means—above all in his eventual marriage to Rita after she reveals she's pregnant with his child—appear in an interesting light. Like Stringer Bell, Dexter is attempting to graduate from one social order to another. Of course, the situation is significantly different given the highly idiosyncratic social order Dexter carries around in his head. For my purposes, one notable question that arises here stems from the fact that the two social orders between which Stringer was trying to move constituted two parts of a larger overarching system. Can this also be the case for Dexter's Code and the larger society in which Dexter moves?

One clear indicator of the relationship between Dexter's Code and the larger society comes when the place Dexter hides the bodies is discovered. As the police piece together the pattern connecting the victims, the public and the media rally behind the killer as an agent of justice. Such sympathy obviously extends only so far—when the man Dexter frames for his murders is killed, his funeral is sparsely attended at best. Nevertheless, the very success of *Dexter* and *24* shows that the public has at least some appetite for vigilante justice.

In this context, it's interesting to note that Harry's status as a police officer is not important only for the know-how he can provide to Dexter in evading capture. Harry is portrayed as having been stymied by legal niceties and actually directs Dexter to kill a murderous pimp who got off on a technicality. When he walks in to see Dexter in the act, however, he is horrified at what he has created and commits suicide shortly thereafter. As with the general public's fickle reaction to Dexter's crimes, one might say that the idea of a serial killer who only kills those who have escaped justice is one thing, but the reality is quite another.

Yet why the extreme reaction? Why not just instruct Dexter to go about his business, but never speak to Harry of it again, for example? It seems to me that what so disturbs Harry is the uncanny sensation of seeing his own darkest impulses embodied before him. In the moment of fury and frustration when the pimp got off, Harry *wanted* to murder him, and now in a very real sense he has, through the murderer that he has painstakingly trained. Seeing one's fantasy realized is often more fun in theory than in practice.

I don't think that Harry is a uniquely bad person, though his loyalty to his son does lead to the sociopathic behavior of training him to kill. The murderous fantasy that Dexter enacts is one that is likely shared by many police officers in such moments of frustration. In Harry's case as in McNulty's obsession with Stringer Bell, however, the dark side of police work shows itself: the fact that it always threatens to become personal. Harry didn't want to kill the pimp out of his pristine devotion to justice, but rather out of his desire to get the fucker who had humiliated him.

Seeing the act of his mentally ill son, who obviously desires violence for its own sake, exposed the uncomfortable truth that he wanted the pimp dead for no reason other than his own personal satisfaction.

Dexter's Code thus represents more than just a clever way of helping him elude capture while harnessing his violence toward some form of justice. It is a kind of systematization of the contradiction at the heart of the police enterprise itself. What motivates the "natural police" such as McNulty is the personal satisfaction of catching criminals and screwing them over, and external discipline is necessary to make sure that impulse toward screwing them over is directed toward something like justice, or at least toward those that society at large also wants to screw over. Though the ostensible goal of law enforcement is to prevent crime, in reality it takes a roundabout route, generally only springing into action after a crime has been committed. In fact, police will often knowingly allow illegal activity to continue so that they can pin a bigger charge on someone, i.e., screw him over even more. This behavior is not so different from that of a street tough who beats someone up to show that he's not to be disrespected. The rogue cop may be offended that the police bureaucracy prefers to keep up appearances and save face rather than pursue real police work, but saving face is exactly what "real" police work is ultimately about—albeit hopefully for society as a whole rather than the police department as an institution.

This discussion puts Dexter's supposedly irresistible violent impulses in a new light. Though Harry presents the Code as a way of coping with them, couldn't one just as easily accuse him of cultivating them, of actively turning Dexter from a disturbed young man into a killer? In that case, even the bloodlust that supposedly cuts Dexter off from society is a social product—not simply a product of his father Harry, but of the police profession that shaped him and that in turn structures so much of society as a whole. (The fact that his killing method is so seemingly antiseptic and passionless, thus echoing the U.S.'s "medicalized" death penalty practices, is another clue that he isn't any more depraved than the law itself.) Dexter thus reverses the usual dilemma of the sociopathic enforcer: he only *thinks* he's acting on his secret violent urges, when in reality he's serving the social demand for justice.

The fact that his service takes the form of murder reveals an unavoidable truth about the demand for justice insofar as it is structured by the institution of the police: it can only destroy. Even granted that it does so in order to avoid even greater destruction, the police institution's tools are essentially all negative: using violence, depriving people of their freedom. The one apparent exception, surveillance, can at best be construed as neutral—though more realistically it attempts to control people through fear. No amount of police spending can rebuild a city, just as no number of invading troops can build a nation. With luck, they can perhaps occasionally open up a space in which something can be built, but they contain no constructive principle in themselves.

The inhuman humanitarian

It would appear, then, that Dexter, perhaps unsurprisingly, does not represent a productive way forward. This is not, however, *solely* for the obvious reason that he's a serial killer. The more fundamental reason is that despite his own self-understanding as being profoundly alienated from mainstream society, his Code is all too closely integrated into it. This mirrors the fundamental tragedy at the heart of Dexter's attempt to become a "normal" person. While he plays the part of the nice, affable guy with some success, he believes that he is somehow incapable of feeling the genuine emotions the people around him feel. Dexter may act friendly, but others actually *like* people; he may offer some token consolation to someone suffering a loss, but others actually *empathize*.

Listening to Dexter's monologues about this gap between his performance and the feelings others supposedly "really" have, it struck me that his problem stems from the very fact that he thinks he's missing out on something. What is a genuinely nice guy, for instance, if not someone who is in the habit of acting like a nice guy? How many people, when consoling a friend, honestly feel empathy in any gut-level level way? He believes that his performance of these rituals when he doesn't "really" feel the corresponding emotion makes him a kind of monster, when in reality everyone else is mostly just going through the motions as well. Other than his secret habit of ritually murdering people, the only thing preventing him from being a "normal" person is his very belief that there is an obstacle.

Where Dexter believes this gap between performance and feeling reveals a problem with him, the final character I'd like to investigate in this book draws the opposite conclusion: "Everybody lies." For Dr. Gregory House, the misanthropic doctor played by Hugh Laurie on the Fox series *House, M.D.*, stereotyped responses reflect bad faith—and the solution is to be sincerely rude at all times. Hearkening, like Dexter, back to the childish schemers, House is a sociopath who rejects the more typical strategy focused on manipulative charm, choosing instead to openly violate social norms and dare people to call him on it.

Despite this affinity with the schemers, however, House does belong firmly in the category of the enforcer. Most obviously, he follows the general pattern of breaking the rules in order to better serve the rules' purpose—in this case, the rules of the hospital where he works and the medical profession in general. The reason for this connection, which as far as I know is unique among medical dramas, is that House's character was based on Sherlock Holmes, who used unconventional methods and his formidable intuition to solve cases the regular police could not. While House has to be an actual medical doctor for the show to make sense, the show similarly portrays his department of diagnostic medicine as the last stop for cases no other doctor has been able to solve. This aspect of the show has been considerably watered down as the years have gone by, as cases are routinely transferred straight from the emergency room to House's department, but it provides an initial frame in which House's no holds barred approach makes sense. (Apparently House's town is overrun with rare diseases in much the same way that Dexter's Miami is plagued by an astonishing number of serial killers.)

Now a natural question arises: if House is so disdainful of his fellow human beings, why does he go to such extreme lengths to save their lives? It certainly isn't because he cares about his patients as individuals—one of the show's running gags is House's unwillingness to have any direct contact with them. A hint can be found in one of House's more memorable quotes, one that cuts to the inhuman aspect at the heart of medical practice in general. Responding to one of his subordinates who, as usual, berates him for his indifference to his patient as a person, House says: "We don't treat patients. We treat diseases."

What appeals to him about medicine isn't the opportunity to help people, but the opportunity to solve extremely difficult puzzles. His investment in his cases really is intensely personal, but it's on the model of the police officer with a personal grudge against a particular criminal. In House's case, though, the criminal who has eluded him happens to be a disease. Given this motivation, House actually avoids everyday medical practice as much as possible, above all in the hospital's free clinic, where all the cases are bound to be routine—and boring.

It is at this point that one can see a fundamental blindness in House's character, similar to Dexter's inability to recognize that "normal" people are also going through the motions. House wants to believe that he's motivated above all by truth and reason, but he only rarely shows himself to be conscious of the fact that his real investment is in the satisfaction that comes from uncovering a well-hidden truth. The reason that he dislikes stereotyped interactions is the same reason he dislikes treating people in the clinic: they're boring and predictable. The same goes for his own patients, as people rather than as medical puzzles—in House's view they're predictably going to lie about something crucial to the diagnosis. One might object that it's actually profoundly interesting that people would be willing to risk their life to stick to a lie, but for House, the reasons that they lie are predictable and boring: above all, people lie to preserve the very stereotyped and sentimental social appearances House disdains.

The people House keeps close to him all somehow avoid this problem of predictability, above all by being willing to put up with such an abusive friend and co-worker, but more interestingly through holding a different set of values from him. Wilson, for example, the show's answer to Holmes's Watson and House's best friend, has gifts that are exactly opposite to House's—his bedside manner is amazing, to the point that House can joke that patients actually *thank* him for telling them they have cancer. Cuddy, the hospital administrator and his mostly unrequited love interest, combines medical talent with a kind of professional ambition totally foreign to House. In choosing co-workers for his department, however, his agenda seems to be more than simply finding a good contrast to bounce off against—he wants the challenge of converting someone to his approach to medicine even when they start from very different standpoints. A recurring theme finds his subordinates successfully making the transition, but then being unable to live with themselves. (In later seasons, in fact, this becomes an easy way for the writers to write a character out of the show.)

A major plotline in the show's third season focuses on his long-time co-worker Foreman's fear that he's becoming "like House" and his desire to escape. The problem starts when Foreman makes a daring diagnostic call that turns out to be wrong, essentially killing a patient. Naturally, he's deeply upset by this, and it causes him to take a more cautious stance that makes House worry Foreman has lost his edge. The truly decisive moment for Foreman, however, is in a later case when he does regain his edge. Due to a complex series of events, two teenage brothers are in a situation where the parents have to make an impossible choice: to save one means allowing the other to die. Foreman comes up with a solution that requires extracting the bone marrow of one of the brothers, even though the brother is so sick that sedating him would endanger his life. Thus Foreman performs the extremely painful procedure without sedation, torturing the boy but successfully saving both brothers' lives. Believing himself to have acted "like House"—that is, like a moral monster who submits human need to medical effectiveness—Foreman submits his resignation after the very act that makes House decide that Foreman does indeed have what it takes.

This conflict comes to a head in a later episode in which Wilson surreptitiously gives House anti-depressants, meaning that House's joy in diagnosis is amplified. In the end, House is deeply satisfied with himself for having "called" a diagnosis based on only the most minimal clues, but he ignores the fact that the diagnosis is untreatable and therefore a teenage girl will die. The whole team is scandalized, but for Foreman, it is especially heinous, and basically confirms to him that House is a moral monster.

In the final episode of the season, House manages to save a woman's life by predicting that she has a heart deformity that has never before been seen—a diagnosis that is extremely satisfying to him. Foreman, on his way out on his last day, confronts House about this satisfaction, saying that House disgusts him, that it's all a game to House, and that Foreman does it (or wants to do it) for the sake of the *people* rather than the intellectual satisfaction. House at first responds simply that the patients don't care about his motivations, only about his effectiveness, but the message of the episode and the season seems to be broader: it's House's satisfaction in diagnosis that makes him so effective. Only by doing medicine for its own sake—which necessarily means directly *enjoying* it—can he ever hope to solve the hopelessly complicated cases that he is faced with.

House's devotion to medicine, then, is completely socio-pathic, in a way that previous characters' devotion to law enforcement can never be: he doesn't care about other people, nor does he care about institutions. All he cares about is his puzzles, to such an extent that he relates to his closest friends as puzzles as well, constantly provoking them as a way of experimenting.

Clearly he requires a unique institutional environment, and the show does present his hospital as a kind of medical utopia. More utopian even than the hospital's apparently limitless budget and lack of concern with insurance, however, is House's only significant intervention on the institutional level, which forms the overarching plot of the first season. In that season, Edward Vogler, a wealthy businessman, makes a huge gift to the hospital in exchange for being made chairman of the board. It quickly becomes clear that his goal isn't entirely altruistic: Vogler wants to use the hospital to run clinical trials for his company. More generally, he wants to get the hospital running like a business, and his first target is House's department, which is of course grossly inefficient. Vogler's attempt to streamline the department quickly becomes a power struggle, with House absolutely refusing to budge. Wilson—who enjoys performing amateur psychoanalysis on House—and others chalk it up to sheer stubbornness on House's part, but it is clear that something deeper is at stake. House won't stand by and let the hospital be submitted to any non-medical demands. In the end, when it has become a choice between keeping House on staff or keeping Vogler's money, Cuddy and the rest of the board choose House.

In the previous examples, the institutions were more than willing to sacrifice the idealistic enforcers when self-preservation demanded it—and no matter what its ostensible external goals are, the goal of every institution is ultimately to preserve itself. House thus didn't just ask his hospital to act in an anti-capitalist way, but in a fundamentally anti-institutional way. What allows this to happen? The simple answer is obviously that it needed to happen for the show to continue, but I think a deeper logic is at work. The various police enforcers can't get their institutions to act against perceived institutional self-interest, because the very purpose of law enforcement is institutional self-preservation in the broadest sense. The police cannot provide an alternative principle to the status quo because the entire point of a police force is to enforce the status quo. House and his hospital— notably a teaching hospital—do offer a potential alternative: not simply "saving lives," but the pursuit of knowledge itself.

Rather than disavowing his personal joy for the sake of conformity to institutional demands, then, House unabashedly demands that the institution conform to his joy—and wins. He gets the institution to advance the most radical and untainted vision of medicine as a search for a diagnosis, simply as an end in itself. For it is clear that saving patients' lives isn't House's direct goal. He is happy to endanger a patient's life, and on the numerous occasions when his incorrect diagnosis nearly kills a patient, he is simply glad to have more information. Saving the patient means that he has beaten the disease, that he has *won*— and if he doesn't, he can always find the diagnosis at autopsy. All things being equal, he prefers a diagnosis for which there's a treatment, but even in this case, it's for the sake of knowledge: if the treatment works, he can know *for sure* that his diagnosis was correct, while the patient's death tells him nothing in specific. Nothing must stand in the way of this quest for knowledge: neither human ethics, nor human sensitivities, nor institutional regulations or demands.

Again, though, there is a sense in which House is blind to his own motivations here. He believes that he is driven by the truth because it's *true*—and, following the previously cited dictum that "truth hurts," he believes that truth must be contrary to human conventions and expectations. Thus he must be rude, for example, because social expectations are a lie.

House is at his worst when this stance leads him to embrace a kind of doctrinaire rationalist approach, for instance deriding Cuddy for picking and choosing among Jewish observances when the only alternatives with any integrity are supposedly either total secular atheism or total fundamentalism. What this ignores is not so much the lived complexity of religious life as the lived complexity of *his own life*. His methodology is not based on sheer reason, but on intuition and above all on serendipitous insights triggered by random conversations. More importantly, his motivation is not the austere vision of objective truth, but the enjoyment of being right. House can't see that he is no exception to his rule that "everybody lies"—most fundamentally to themselves.

This blindness leads me to conclude that even House, who in many respects I regard as the most promising TV sociopath, is not rigorously sociopathic enough. By rejecting social convention in principle, he is still allowing it to dominate his life, if only negatively. True freedom from the law does not mean breaking the law at every opportunity—if you are truly free from the law, you are free even to take actions that happen to be in conformity to it. Thus I would claim that House, who combines so many aspects of the schemer and the enforcer, needs to add in the seductive, manipulative skills of the climber. After all, if social conventions are all lies in any case, what's the harm of dishonestly using them to make—or keep—friends?

House does attempt to make use of social conventions at times, but primarily in the service of "happiness," understood as something like a normal life. In the most recent season as of this writing, for example, he finally had his chance to date Cuddy and tried his best to be the attentive boyfriend she expected him to be (despite having known him for decades). Other seasons have had him struggle with the drug addiction brought on by a leg injury that leaves him in continual pain. In all these cases, a pattern recurs: House believes that achieving "happiness" and maintaining his unique gift for medicine are incompatible. After his drug addiction leads to hallucinations and forces him into rehab, for instance, House believes that he must leave behind medicine in order to stay off the drugs—a variation on the normal pattern where House will find some kind of solution to his chronic pain and immediately abandon it when his resulting sunny disposition seems to hurt his diagnostic skills.

What draws me to House, despite the show's poor writing and repetitiousness, is that he always winds up choosing his gift over "happiness" in the end. Only in rare moments, however, can he admit to himself why he is doing so: namely, because his gift satisfies him more than "happiness" ever could. The reason most often offered actually follows the logic of the climber: he wants to be "special" in some way, rather than being merely ordinary. For me, this leaves the show in constant danger of shifting toward a more cynical vision of life, one where "happiness" and the pursuit of truth are necessarily incompatible *and therefore we must choose the lie*. House as the noble bearer of the burden of truth would thus serve only to reinforce the necessity of the equally noble lie on which society is structured.

To their credit, the writers almost never take things in that direction, but they are equally reluctant to openly embrace the view that House's approach to life is *better* than "happiness." Instead, viewers are treated to endless reflections from House's friends about how he's afraid to be happy, etc., etc. These reflections, which probably present what we're supposed to take as the "official viewpoint" of the show, place House's struggles within the basic framework discussed in the introduction, whereby the sociopath is either redeemed through his embrace of "normal" family life or punished through his inability to adapt to it.

Perhaps this framework was necessary to appeal to a mass audience—in fact, I suspect that *House* may have turned out to be a much better show had its creators pitched it to HBO rather than a broadcast network. In any case, however, the end result is that despite challenging the fantasy of the enforcer in significant ways, he nevertheless remains the exceptional individual who breaks society's rules in order to reinforce them. What's more, the primary ways that he challenges the fantasy of the enforcer is by incorporating elements of the previous classes of sociopath, namely the schemer's childlike enjoyment and the climber's desire to be special or superior.

House thus represents a kind of recapitulation of all the main themes of the fantasy sociopath. Though the show sometimes pushes the boundaries of that fantasy in a more authentically subversive direction, it ultimately fails to break through to something new. At the same time, House's character also seems to me to point in a particularly clear way toward what is possibly redemptive in the fantasy of the sociopath, and it is to that potential that I now turn.

Conclusion:
Redeeming the fantasy sociopath

Is there anything redemptive about the fantasy of the TV sociopath? There is at least one significant benefit: it clearly points toward a feeling of dissatisfaction with a broken society. It reflects the widespread perception that contemporary society is alienating and unjust, led by self-aggrandizing elites interested in (and competent at) little more than perpetuating their own power. As a cultural diagnosis, this seems to me to be a good first approximation. Even if there are pockets of hope, late capitalist society is disturbingly destructive and amoral, demanding ever more of the many while enriching the few. I have perhaps focused on *The Wire* to a degree that is disproportionate to its relatively small audience, but its bleak vision of our social system differs only in sophistication from that of the other shows, not in kind. Essentially all the TV shows focused on sociopathic characters portray the world as some variation on *The Wire*'s Baltimore—even the fantasy worlds of the vulgar cartoons take it for granted that the world is going to shit.

As a kind of folk social analysis, then, the fantasy of the sociopath seems to be fairly serviceable. On the level of possible responses to a broken society, however, it seems much less promising, because nearly all the points of identification it offers serve to reinforce the social system. This is clearest in the case of the climber, who accepts society's standards for success to the greatest possible extent, but it is also present in the enforcer, whose goal is ultimately to force society to be true to itself. In neither case is there any possible outside point of reference. The schemer may initially seem to escape this problem through their childlike enjoyment, but this potential "outside" is presented as a kind of unsustainable chaos. At best, the antics of Homer Simpson and Eric Cartman serve as a kind of release valve for the pressures of adult responsibility, but they're a fun indulgence, not something you'd base your life on.

The same might be said of the more serious TV sociopaths as well. Certainly I'm not likely to imitate Cartman in my everyday life, but there's little chance that I would imitate Don Draper or Jack Bauer, either. I might like to *imagine* that I would ruthlessly and creatively exploit opportunities for advancement or that I would do whatever it took to save lives—but in reality, I would likely bumble awkwardly through such situations, much as I do through my everyday life.

Most viewers would surely admit the same thing, but that awareness masks a much deeper level of fantasy: namely, the fantasy that *there are* real-life Don Drapers or Jack Bauers. In reality, of course, social mobility in the Western world is incredibly low and declining, while the persistent failure of the U.S. military to achieve its ostensible goals abroad indicates that we don't have a reliable way to produce superheroes in the Jack Bauer mold. What the fantasy of characters like Don Draper and Jack Bauer provides us with, however, is the hope that our system is still somehow a meritocracy and still somehow competent at fulfilling its baseline promises (such as physical safety).

Yet at this deepest level, the fantasy is also at its most unambitious. What kind of fantasy is it to say that people can get a satisfying job, *if* they are capable of amazingly ruthless behavior unrelated to the ostensible skill set required to do that job? How reassuring is it to learn that the U.S. will be free of terrorist attacks, as long as there's *one guy* willing to take it to the limit and openly defy every law and authority? The candidness of this fantasy is remarkable in much the same way as was the propaganda in favor of Reagan's "trickle-down economics"—even if it works as advertised, it's still only going to produce a "trickle."

At this point, the grim social analysis appears in a more insidious light. While basically accurate, these shows' bleak outlook may serve to produce cynicism and fatalism, such that the "less bad" option represented by the meager compensation Don Draper and Jack Bauer offer may be positively appealing. Thus even a correct diagnosis of society's failings can serve to reinforce our Stockholm Syndrome-like identification with it.

Truly this is a society that succeeds by failing. It seems like this should make it easier to get away from, but it paradoxically makes it much more difficult, because it concedes virtually all criticism in advance. The result is a strange variation on the model of the asshole who cuts in line and then dares someone to call him on it: if someone does call him out, he'll openly concede that it's unfair that he jumped the queue, but if he hadn't, someone else would've come along and cut in any case. Another model can be found in a scene from *The Simpsons*, drawn from an episode in which Homer has accidentally created a highly addictive hybrid of tomatoes and tobacco called tomacco. A tobacco company learns of his discovery and offers him a huge amount of money for the product, believing it provides a new way to hook children on their products. When his idealistic daughter Lisa urges him to turn down the money and destroy all the tomacco plants to avoid unleashing a social plague, he responds, "I wish I could make a difference, Lisa, but I'm just one man."

If even the social critique implicit in these shows can be mobilized in defense of the system, what's left? Are there any elements of the fantasy of the sociopath that can be used for another purpose in a way that wouldn't immediately collapse back into reinforcing our collective Stockholm Syndrome? The answer may well turn out to be no, but I believe there are at least a few elements in these fantasies that provide something other than, or at least separable from, social reinforcement—in fact, there *must* be at least some such elements, if only to keep these shows from being boring propaganda.

Among the schemers, it seems to me that the most redeeming

quality is their childlike joy. While their plots to screw over their friends anticipate the world of adult competition all too clearly, and while their goals are often petty and stupid, the characters in this category all experience moments of satisfaction that can only be called "innocent." For me an iconic moment is Cartman's joy at experiencing the attractions of Casa Mamita even as the police descend upon him. He has ruthlessly victimized his friend Butters in order to enjoy what amounts to an average Mexican restaurant with a few cheap gimmicks—but in his moment of satisfaction, he still seems somehow innocent.

These moments of pure enjoyment stand in sharp contrast to much adult consumption, which is often motivated by a desire to signal one's social status or else by a sense of obligation that can make entertainment into a chore. Even cynical adults have moments like that, though they tend to dismiss them as pathetic or somehow embarrassing—for instance, the simple joy in getting one's computer to do something in *just the right way*. Why should we be ashamed of our enjoyment, though? Why can't we become like little children in this way?

In terms of the climbers, I would first single out their creativity and willingness to take risks. There is much to dislike about Don Draper, but in his moments of sociopathic genius, he is exhilarating to watch. Similarly, Stringer Bell is shockingly naïve about the social circles he wishes to enter and blind to how much of a typical gangster he remains, and yet his willingness to reimagine the drug trade as a non-violent, mutually beneficial enterprise is a bold and creative response to his disadvantageous position. Though both are acting ultimately for their own advancement within the given system, there's no reason why that kind of risky creativity could not be devoted to other ends.

Even outside of their more creative moments, however, we could learn much from the climbers' unsentimental instrumentalization of social norms. Peggy Olsen provides good examples here, as when she simply *asks* to be assigned a large office that has been laying dormant for weeks. (One can easily imagine that the other characters were waiting for the bosses to assign it, or felt it would be rude or insensitive to ask, etc.) On the larger scale, I could picture someone responding to a situation like Peggy's unexpected pregnancy by retreating back to the shelter of home, either by going back to live with her mother or by shaming the father of the baby into marrying her. Both responses would mean that she was viewing her situation through the eyes of society's demands rather than her own satisfaction—in the first case, viewing it as a sin for which she must atone, or in the second, taking it as a sign that she must fulfill her duty of getting married and raising a family. Yet instead she chooses to return to the creative work that satisfies her, which represents a refusal of society's tendency to use our felt obligations as blackmail.

In both of these examples, Peggy shows what it looks like to stop acting in a self-undermining way. This can happen either preemptively, as in cases of convincing ourselves not to even ask for what we want, or after the fact, as when we believe we deserve some kind of "punishment." Her position as a woman in an overwhelmingly male-dominated environment forces her to test out the maxim of "ask and ye shall receive." The maxim doesn't always hold true, but it is an absolute certainty that if you don't ask, you will never receive—there is no omniscient boss who will reward you for your quiet hard work. Asking may turn out to be overly bold, but as with line-cutting, there is no set punishment for violating that social norm. The strategy of breaking a norm and daring someone to call it out works for the queue-jumper, so why not for us? As with the examples of Don and Stringer, Peggy's instrumentalization here is geared toward advancing in the existing system, but this strategy could equally serve other ends.

Finally, from the enforcers, I would draw out their dedication to a goal more important than normal life. In the case of the law enforcement examples, they are fundamentally deluded about the nature of their goal, but House's goal of tracking down a diagnosis—and by extension, of pursuing knowledge by unraveling complex puzzles—seems like a worthy one to me, and other similarly worthy ones could be imagined.

The inherent satisfaction that these characters take from pursuing their goals, most often to the detriment of their conventional happiness, seems to me to indicate that what is most often at stake in happiness isn't any kind of satisfaction outside the satisfaction of conformity itself. This assessment of happiness is perhaps clearest in the case of Dexter, who believes himself to be incapable of normal emotional attachments but wants the trappings of a normal life nevertheless. Yet one can also approach this negatively: why should someone like McNulty, for example, have ever gotten married and had children in the first place? If police work is everything to him, why even take on these extraneous obligations, other than out of a sense that it's what "everybody" does?

Thus, while many of the enforcers are portrayed as nobly sacrificing their families, they also suggest the possibility of a point of view in which it's no sacrifice at all. Given the way that family provides both a potent means for the system to blackmail us and a supposedly irrefutable excuse for engaging in all kinds of destructive behavior, questioning the value of the family unit may well be one of the most necessary tasks for those who want to break the hold of our current broken society over our imaginations.

What these reflections point toward is the figure of a more radically sociopathic sociopath, who combines the joy of the schemer and the single-mindedness of the enforcer with the creativity, persuasiveness, and unsentimental outlook of the climber. Such sociopaths could use the norms of our present social order without being bound by them and could form relationships based on enjoyment and the desire to *know* the other person rather than out of sentiment and obligation. I would even dare to say that radical sociopaths of this type could very well be the ones to invent a "better game" than the stultifying game of chess adult life under late capitalism has become, drawing people in through the persuasiveness of their very way of being in the world—and that's because it seems to me that many of the great cultural innovators, such as Jesus, Buddha, or Socrates, have been sociopathic in just the sense I'm describing.

Such sociopaths would doubtless make for a great TV show, but we can't expect our society to create them for us. To find sociopaths of this kind, we must seek them out in the real world—or else become them.

Contemporary culture has eliminated both the concept of the public and the figure of the intellectual. Former public spaces – both physical and cultural – are now either derelict or colonized by advertising. A cretinous anti-intellectualism presides, cheerled by expensively educated hacks in the pay of multinational corporations who reassure their bored readers that there is no need to rouse themselves from their interpassive stupor. The informal censorship internalized and propagated by the cultural workers of late capitalism generates a banal conformity that the propaganda chiefs of Stalinism could only ever have dreamt of imposing. Zer0 Books knows that another kind of discourse – intellectual without being academic, popular without being populist – is not only possible: it is already flourishing, in the regions beyond the striplit malls of so-called mass media and the neurotically bureaucratic halls of the academy. Zer0 is committed to the idea of publishing as a making public of the intellectual. It is convinced that in the unthinking, blandly consensual culture in which we live, critical and engaged theoretical reflection is more important than ever before.